Go with the Flow

Go with

Cho Hunhyun

the Flow

How the Great Master of Go Trained His Mind

INFLUENTIAL

Cho Hunhyun

As the most respected Go master in Korea, Japan, and China, he has rewritten the modern history of Go by winning the largest number of victories. Becoming a professional go player at the age of nine, he went to Japan to be taught by Kensaku Segoe, one of the best Go masters in Japan for nine years.

Starting with the first championship of the Ing Cup in 1989, which is dubbed the 'Go Olympics' he has achieved a grand slam for the first time in Go history by sweeping up championship trophies of all three major tournaments (the Ing Cup, the Fujistu Cup World Go Championship, the Tongyang Securities Cup) for five years afterward. He became the oldest winner of an international competition at the age of 50, which is the age that most professional Go players consider retirement. His strict self-discipline enabled him to make such a remarkable achievement that still remains as an unbroken record.

As a member of the National Assembly, he has taken the lead of non-governmental diplo-macy between Korea and China and also been active in various fields such as lecture and writing. More than a hundred thousand copies of his book, *Go with the Flow*, were sold right after publication, ascending to the bestseller spot in Korea and being translated and published in Japan and China as well.

This is an important addition to body of books in English about Go. We in the West now have many books and teachers that can instruct us in how to play the game, but few that tell us what it is like to be a top Go player.

Cho Hunhyun 9P does this with great openness, telling us his emotions, his feelings and perceptions, as he goes through the very taxing life necessary to have a chance to be a champion. He recounts trading an ordinary childhood for a childhood devoted to the game, trading life at home for life with a teacher in a foreign country, Japan, pursuing a career where one's merit is measured anew with each move, surviving the inevitable descent from the summit as he lost one title then another, some to his own student.

Perhaps most notable is Cho's recounting of the story of his relationship with his teacher. Segoe Kensaku 9P was one of the more important teachers in 20th Century Go in Japan, based primarily on the reputations of his three pupils, Cho, Utaro Hashimoto 9P, and Go Seigen 9P. Cho's story of the seemingly cold but deep bond he had with Segoe, the lessons he learned, and the circumstances of Segoe's life and death, are something well worth reading, and not material that I have seen anywhere else. Cho goes on to describe his relationship with his only student, successor Korean champion Lee Changho 9P, which shared much with the student-teacher connection Cho had with Segoe.

What emerges is the portrait of a remarkable man, who has had a rich, full life and wide-ranging interests, but all concentrated in a sense by the lens of Go. It was a joy to read.

– Andrew Okun, President, America Go Association

Cho Hunhyun studied Go in Japan as a child prodigy, after which he returned to Korea to become one of the greatest players in Go history. Cho's unique life experience makes him the perfect person to introduce us to the Go scene in Korea and Japan.

In *Go with the Flow*, Cho writes of his struggles to become a better Go player. There are many episodes about players who earned Cho's respect, giving us a fascinating collection of stories about the best Go players of the 20th century. Cho talks of his friend Jimmy Cha, who was a prominent player when he lived in America. This book can be enjoyed by anyone who has an interest in Go or Asian culture.

– Michael Redmond, Professional Go Player

Go with the Flow is a collection of anecdotes from the life of one of the game's great masters. With each story, Mr. Cho relates the lessons he learned in his career as a professional player – patience, poise, humility, how to cope with loss – to his philosophy on life outside the Go board. "The strength to think", writes Cho, "is the only beacon that helps one get through life. Along the journey, we learn more about ourselves…"

Anyone interested in the modern history of the game will find something to love from Cho's insightful memoir.

– Will Lockhart, Film Director, The Surrounding Game

It's thrilling to read Cho Hunhyun recount the stories of some of his most famous victories, but I was most touched by how much he dealt with the sadness, frustration, and loss he experienced in his career. Cho's life story brings together some of the most important and vivid figures in 20th Century Go, from his formative years training in Japan as a teenager to his return to Korea and rediscovery of the disregard for supposedly ideal shape that would came to define Korean go. He writes touchingly of his relationships with his austere but generous teacher, Segoe Kensaku, with 'monster' Fujisawa Shuko who was madly in love with life, and with his remote and exacting student, Lee Changho, who would rise to defeat him in a series of maddening half-point victories. Cho is candid about how miserable it is for pros to review a game they've lost, despite the calm composure they maintain on the outside: Go players review games because it's vital, not because it ever becomes easy. Cho's thoughts on the importance of physical exercise, a persistent and optimistic drive to find the best solutions possible, and making time for solitude are relevant to all of us.

– Nate Eagle, Co-Director, 2018 U.S. Go Congress

Mr. Cho Hunhyun 9P, became professional at the age of nine (the youngest player to become a professional). After winning his first title in 1975 he dominated not just the Korean Go scene until 1990.

Winning the first Ing Cup, gave the Korean Go scene a lot of prestige worldwide. This book gives you many nice stories and memories of Mr. Cho.

Best are the stories where he gives the reader inside information about professional go, and how to become and get stronger as professional go player.

– Antonius Claasen, Reporter, European Go Federation

Table of Contents

Learning from Go

I don't know anything else but Go. I was only five when I took my first steps over the threshold of a Go club. My father took my hands in his and brought me down to that place in my hometown of Mokpo. Ever since then and now- I am way over 60- it has all been about Go and nothing else.

I never received formal education nor had a corporate job. My acquaintances are limited to those in the Go community. I did not get to live the expected, predictable yet colorful experiences that most people have. Preparing for college admission, competing for jobs, agonizing about making the right career move, being overwhelmed by the feeling electricity when falling in love, and dealing with the stress of corporate life…I have missed out on these spectacular events of an ordinary life.

However, it doesn't mean I don't know about life. Within my universe of Go, I believe I have had my fair share of passion and indifference, love and hatred, hope and despair, success and failure, loyalty and dishonesty. My life may have appeared too monotonous and simple to the eyes of others, but to me, it was an equally, if not the most, vibrant and eventful life I could have lived.

I gave up my childhood to learn Go. I lived away from home when kids my age lived with their parents and got to be 'kids.' From the age of eleven to eighteen, I lived in Japan to train for Go. My parents did not follow me. At an early age, I had already swept medals in Go championships in Korea, and the winning streak took me all the way to win titles in world championships. But, at only forty-three, I had to confront my student and lose every single one of my title to him. It was bitter because I was defeated, but sweet because I was proud of my student.

All my life, I have crashed to the ground and climbed my way up again, over and over. One would think that after so many victories or defeats, one would become thick-skinned. But, losing still stings. Now that I am getting older and clumsier, I have been losing more games.

And yet I still play Go. I used to play to win, but now for the love of it. Once dubbed a natural winner, the realization that life is not always about winning came when I took a step back. What matters most is to do your best on the path you have chosen.

Most of us, unfortunately, choose to think in ways that make us insecure and are quick to assume that we have failed in life. We let little things upset us and blowing them out of proportion; we worry about things in the future that may never happen; we have a hard time getting over life's small setbacks; we let trivial things hurt our feelings and crash our morale.

Heaven or hell? It all depends on how one looks at things. In my early days, I was too young to realize it. But now, I appreciate the saying. It took years of conditioning- allowing myself to look at life's unanticipated events from a different angle- so that I can move on. I was in great agony when my only student took my championship titles one by one. But, I thought, if those titles were meant to be taken by someone someday, it was perhaps better for me to see none other than my own student take the honor from me. I felt better immediately. I contemplated about retirement when I lost all of my titles and failed to make it even to the preliminary match. I felt at ease, however, when I realized that I had hit rock bottom and the only way was up.

It all comes down to how one chooses to think. Everyday cannot be perfect. Good days and bad days take turns in getting washed up the shore. Infancy is the only worry-free days we get to enjoy and it is over in a fleeting moment. We are soon driven to deal with life- a continuum of troubles and distress. So how does one cope with life-long distress?

This is where shifting perspectives makes all the difference. One needs to change the way one thinks to carry on with the rest of the days in one's life. Reformulate how one thinks. Every day must be filled with thoughts that fuel one to carry on happily; thoughts that emanate optimism, creativity, self-confidence, and sound judgement. When one transforms the way one thinks, it triggers a chain reaction in one's behavior and in the daily routine, which all weaves into a story that ends on the right note. The mind is the most powerful force that brings out the best in oneself.

The objective of Go is to control more territory than one's opponent. It resembles our life in that respect. Every day, we make a fierce move to expand our own "turf," whatever that may mean to each of us. But, with what thought in mind? We need to remind ourselves of the great power of thinking as we take a step forward. Carry on and visualize the wider ground we deserve. Make the effort to place each stone in the best possible position the board.

We are already the winner of our lives as long as we have fought with all our might.

In the spring of 2015
Cho Hunhyun

"All it took me was to walk into the forest of my thoughts,
where the twigs of my thoughts led me to the answers.
The answers were already there, expecting me."

Chapter 1

How Go
Masters
Think

THE FIFTH AND
THE FINAL DECIDING GAME

It was at 9:30 in the morning, September 5, 1989. I was spacing out, sitting in the bed in my hotel room in Singapore. I had come down with the flu soon after I landed in the country, which left my skin extremely sensitive and annihilated my taste buds that I was forcing the hot soup and bread down my throat. The final round of the tournament was just about to begin. My mouth was dry and I was getting into a stew. Just before the Final fifth of the Ing Changki Cup, I closed my eyes and tried to control my breathing. I took a long breath out and the images of the past few months passed before my eyes as if recalled from a magic lantern; the Ing Cup tour card, which I secured as the only Korean Go player; the quarterfinal round with Koichi Kobayashi and the semifinal match with Rin Kaiho, in both of which I was cornered for the eleventh hour before winning by a narrow margin; ten days in China that felt like purgatory; exhaustingly managing the final fourth round and miraculously ending the game in a tie.

The Ing Changki Cup, or Ing Cup for short, is a professional international Go championship launched by Ing Changki himself, a Taiwanese-born billionaire who generously contributed his own fortune to creating the tournament. I was among the finalists in the inaugural 1989 tournament. At around the same time, the Fujitsu Cup, another international Go championship, also one of the first in the world, was created in Japan. But, it was no match to the Ing Cup, both in scale and significance. The Ing Cup was the Go Olympics, held every four years and the prize money for the winner was a colossal amount of 400,000 dollars. Every year the 'Go Olympics' was held, the world was obsessed to find out who was going to win the biggest cash prize ever in the history of Go championship.

The Ing Cup was created to promote the Chinese Go, which has always taken pride in being identified as the country of origin of Go; but its longtime dilemma was that it was always overshadowed by Japan's leadership in international Go. And then something unexpected happened at the 1985 inaugural China-Japan Supermatches. Nie Weiping, from China, rode on a 11 game winning streak in the first three tournaments playing against top Japanese players.

China was hoping to continue to pick up steam and solidify its place as the world's ultimate Go power house. The Ing Cup was supposed to be the venue for the greater glory of the state. And China wanted the world to know that it was going all for it; half of the players in the Ing Cup were either from China or had Chinese background. Two thirds of the rest were from Japan and only two Koreans; Cho Chikun and myself. Cho Chikun having qualified as professional player through Nihon Ki-in, the Japan Go Association made me the sole player representing Korean Go.

In this masterplan, I was included to be the stalking horse. The host of the Ing Cup had tossed the tournament ticket with my name on it up in the air; whether I caught it or not, they couldn't care less. It was insulting, but I had no choice but to take it. It was the opportunity that I had to seize in order to learn from world-class players even if it meant coming home completely crushed. But, something unexpected happened; to everyone's shock, I made it to the final round. My humble role was to just show up and fill in the assortment of Go players the organizer had created for their plan.

The eyes of the world now shifted from the Sino-Japan competition to the battle Korea was waging against China. Neither could afford to lose; China desperately needed a victory. Its pride as the first country to play Go was at stake. Korea saw it as a golden opportunity to finally take a step into the center of the stage, and remove its reputation of being a 'nobody' in international Go.

For ultimate victory, I had to win the first three rounds out of five in the finals. The finals didn't start until five months after the semifinal was over. Just a few weeks before the first round of the finals, the organizer informed us that all of the five rounds of the finals was going to take place in China. It meant that the Chinese player was going to enjoy the home ground advantage while his opponents would have to risk losing

in the Chinese playing field. It was a complete nonsense. The Korean team made a strong objection and convinced the organizer to set up three rounds in China, and two in a third country.

Even so, I realized I was still behind the eight ball as I was on my way to China. This was happening at a time when we referred to China as "the communist China." With no diplomatic ties between Korea and China, there was no direct flight between the two countries. It was a two full day trip to China; I had to go to Hong Kong to get my visa, and take every mode of transportation, in addition to the plane, ship, and the train, just to get to Hangzhou. By the time I made it to the hotel, I was completely exhausted, barely able to hold up myself.

To make matters worse, tension in the communist state was suffocating. The atmosphere was already warlike the second I was getting off the plane. The first thing I noticed was the MIG jet fighters lined up on the runway and Chinese security police was everywhere. The spacious and pleasant look of the hotel was not enough to conceal the heavy and stifling air. Whenever I left the hotel, I was always followed by the security police as if they were my shadow. Pitch-darkness and eerie silence fell when the hands of the clock pointed 6 o'clock in the evening. I was hardly breathing, not because of the pressure of the coming match but because of the stress I got from the surroundings.

The first round of the finals began under this circumstances. It ended with a lucky win for me, attributable not to my good play but to my opponent, Nie Weiping, who was in a bad shape. He had been under tremendous pressure to win and was crumbling under the weight of all the expectation he had been receiving. Worse, he had a heart condition that required an oxygen mask to be ready nearby at all times in case of emergency.

Nie Weiping won the second and the third round which took place a few days apart. I lost, not because he was better than me but because I was having a nervous breakdown, intimidated by the hostile mood in the communist China. I was so ready to leave China after only being in the country for a week. I was breaking down mentally. My nerves were in shreds.

The news of Nie Weiping's winning streak was all over China and the country was assuming victory, prepared to pop the champagne, while I was quietly packing to go home. China showed no mercy for the defeated even on the day I was leaving. The Chinese government stopped me from leaving for Hong Kong, saying that there was something wrong with my documents. I was afraid that I would be detained forever in China.

I went through hell and high water to get on board of a ship to Hong Kong. Only then did I feel a breath of fresh air in my body. I survived!

Four months later, the last two rounds of the finals were held in Singapore. The goddess of victory seemed to smile at the Chinese player. Nie Weiping was glowing with confidence at the dinner reception as if he too, felt that victory was on his side. "Obviously, a Chinese player deserves to win the world's biggest tournament hosted by the Chinese. Who else? The championship cup is mine!" he said.

By contrast, I had only one goal on my mind. Never let it be an easy win for anyone. I'll hang on and finish the final round. To that end, I had to win the fourth round. When Nie Weiping and I were sitting face-to-face to play the game, I could tell that he was under as much pressure as I was. He was not the same confident man whom I saw at the dinner reception. We were evenly matched. But I realized, whoever had the unwavering focus until the last was going to be the winner.

I used the same opening strategy that I had used earlier in the second round, hoping to stand a chance to win by not repeating the same mistake as before. Nie Weiping and I took turns moving our stones, advancing at a controlled pace. It was a tight game and we were both very nervous. Every move made by the Black seemed to gain the upper hand, but only to be quickly reversed by the White and vice versa. It was going to be neck and neck for a while.

An opportunity finally came for me to give it a go. By the time there was barely any empty space had remained on the board, Nie Weiping made a small but critical mistake and I didn't hesitate to finish the game. After tallying the scores when the game was over, I was declared the winner: I won by one point.

I managed to stay and continue on to the fifth round! I was more excited about nothing else but this. To me, giving up was more shameful than being defeated. The last thing I wanted was for people to see me, the grandmaster of Go in Korea, lose grace and dignity in a game against a top player in China. I was now back in the game. The previous four rounds didn't mean anything anymore. The fifth round was all that mattered now.

The historical match began. Nie Weiping started to work his way outward, building castles in the center of the board, while I focused on attacking the periphery, gouging out corners. Nie Weiping was gaining on me fending off every attack. Halfway through the game, I got distracted and I couldn't figure out my next move. Nie Weiping would never miss a chance like this: He kept striking back, cornering me. His fatal blows were by a hair's breadth away and I was frantically trying to keep my head above water. Was he going to finish me off after dragging me around? A small voice in my head sweet-talked me to give up and take a rest since I had done everything I could.

Suddenly, I looked up and saw Nie Weiping's face. I quickly snapped out of it. Nie Weiping was completely immersed in the game. Whenever he placed his stone on the board, he seemed to even forget breathing. We both needed to win. He was under as much pressure as I was, even with his heart condition. It wasn't any easier for him, if not far worse. Yet, he persevered, holding his own against me.

Wake up. It's not over yet. Stay focused. And keep thinking. I said to myself.

I let my mind walk into the forest of my thoughts. Slowing down, taking one step at a time. I was beginning to get my breathing rhythm back and felt comfortable once again. Everything around me disappeared. Everyone was gone; Nie Weiping and the staff members. Feelings of anxiety, nervousness, and even my ambition to win vanished. There was just the two of us left: Go and I. At that moment of absolute relinquishment, I was able to see very clearly: the perfect point to place my stone!

I heard the timekeeper's 10-second countdown from a distance. One, two, three, four, five, six…. I got back my sense of reality. When the time-keeper said seven, I placed my stone with confidence. It was the 129th move.

That move changed everything. I began to take the initiative. Nie Weiping was busy to ward off my attacks. Soon, there was no place for him to run away. When I made my 145th move with certainty, Nie Weiping dropped his head and placed two stones on the board. He was resigning.

"Hunhyun won!"

I realized that I had finally won when Korean cheering squad in the viewing room burst out shouts of victory. Ah, I won. I won!

On that day, Korean Go catapulted to the top of the world. It was a historic event for the Korean Go community. Riding on the momentum, Korean players won the next three straight Ing Cup championships; the 2nd, 3rd, and the 4th Ing Cup. Korea gained dominance in international Go over a short period of time.

The final round of that Ing Cup is still much talked about. In particular, people still wonder about the 129th move which put me back into the game. "How did you come up with that killer move with only 10 seconds left to save yourself?"

"I have no idea. I still don't know." My reply has always been the same. All I did was to surrender myself to the forest of my thoughts. I didn't find the answer. My thoughts led me to it.

The game of Go is akin to life. The feelings of joy, anger, sorrow, and happiness that we experience as we go through life are evoked while playing Go. In this sense, this particular board game can help us put all the complex and intricate issues of our real life into perspective. Tackling these issues will not be easy, but there can be no knots that cannot be untied.

Playing Go is a process of finding answers. When a player sits in front of the board, the first thing to do is to plan out the game to win. The player, however, must not expect the plan to always work because the opponent is essentially doing the same; planning elaborate schemes and strategies to win. For this reason, interception is played out constantly on the Go board. Players are cornered by unanticipated moves; to save themselves, they must pursue every avenue to survive.

In this respect, every single professional Go player is a master in problem solving. To Go players, every problem in the world is bound to have a solution. We are trained over and over, from an early age, to challenge ourselves with seemingly impossible problems but we have always found the way out. It does not always have to be me. There is always someone else who could solve the problem. Problems are bound to be solved as long as the player has the tenacity to grapple with them until they are solved.

That tenacity is empowered by thinking. 'Thinking' is an abstract con-

Whether it be on the brink of a cliff, caught in a trap,

and pay an arm and a leg for one's own mistake,

a Go player must do one's best until the end.

cept that includes many qualities necessary to solve problems; staying optimistic about finding the solutions; willing to see the problems through to the end; employing every means- knowledge, common sense, logic, creative ideas- to solve the problems. I refer to this type of thinking as, the 'Go masters' way of thinking' because this is how a Go master thinks.

There is no problem that cannot be solved. Clues may not be visible right away and the problem may seem to get worse at every attempt to solve it. But, there is always a solution to a problem as long as one has the will to solve it. Even with utmost endeavors, if the ideal solution is out of the reach, take the second best solution. If the second best is not feasible, take the third best solution. Of course the solutions do not necessarily result in what one hopes for. Along the way, one may be forced to make concessions, compromises, or give up and move on to other plans. But, in one way or another, these are all part of the solutions.

It is imperative, however, that the initiative has to come from one-self. So many people choose to walk away from the problem instead of attempting to tackle it head-on. Rather than making real efforts to fig-ure their way out, they give in prematurely to the stress of anxiety and takes on the devil-may-care attitude, leaving things to their own course. It would be the same as placing one's stones on random points when feeling completely stuck in Go.

Professional Go players never act in such a way. They fiercely carry on to come up with the next move knowing that the overtime countdown is going to begin soon. They make every move count until they are forced to resign, and even when they know, by intuition, that they are going to lose the game. Whether the move is deemed as the best, a good one, a bad one or an overreaction, all move made by the player is the outcome of intensive thinking.

In Go, there are goals to achieve, logics to apply and rules to abide by. This aspect of Go makes professional Go players strategists. A player must have a strategy, be tactful, and read ahead before placing the stones. Every move must count.

There is a winner and a loser in Go. A player must come up with every possible move to win no matter what. Whether it be on the brink of a cliff, caught in a trap, and pay an arm and a leg for one's own mistake, a Go player must do one's best until the end.

Essentially, we are all playing our own Go to make it through the day. If we have placed one stone a day, how far have we come today? Are we still in the opening or have we made it to the middle of the game? Or have we made the very last bet in the game? No matter where we are, our game is not over unless we have filled the entire board with stones, or until someone resigns. There is always hope, no matter what.

The real problem is when the determination to navigate out from trouble is lacking, or when one chooses to quit thinking. Excuses, such as 'there was nothing else I could do,' or 'I didn't have any choice,' are unacceptable in Go. Opportunities as well as mistakes all derive from oneself. Winning is electrifying while losing is bitter. But every victory or even failure resets the learning curve. The strength to think is the only beacon that helps one get through life. Along the journey, we learn more about ourselves and discover happiness.

THE EMPTY TRIANGLE

People called me a Go whiz. From the age of five, I have been in and out of Go clubs, offering advice to my father on his moves and beating most of the adults who played in those Go clubs. Passing the Professional Qualification Tournament at the age of nine, I became the youngest professional Go player in the world.

I remember how whenever I placed a stone, the spectators opened their eyes wide in amazement and let out an exclamation. "How does this boy come up with such an extraordinary move?" Wherever I went, people called me Go prodigy. In retrospect, I was not a genius nor a master of Go. I was just being myself- a free thinker.

Adults who played Go were under the heavy influence of the Japanese pattern back then. Pattern in Go means the standard sequence of placing stones which has been time-tested to be the optimal to attack or defend. In Go, stones are placed according to certain formulas and patterns. But, I could not have known them. I was only a child. All I knew was that I wanted to win. I wanted to win so much so that I started to think of any move and every move that seemed to make sense- refreshingly odd moves that grownups would never in a million years come up with.

Later when I went to Japan and was introduced to the pattern for the first time in my life, I was embarrassed because it was only then that I realized how untamed my moves had been. Without knowing the basics of Go, I had played it like a bull in a china shop. I learned the importance of knowing the basics as I was brutally crushed over and over by Japanese Go students.

However, once a player has a solid foundation in the basics, it is necessary to go back being an unleashed horse. The game is over at the moment the player decides to play only by the patterns. How can a player win when the moves are so obvious and can be easily anticipated by the opponent? Go is a mind game, ideas of two players fighting against each other. A player must think differently to play effectively.

At the Ing Cup, I pulled off the 'empty triangle,' twice in the first round of the semi-finals. Empty triangle is formed when three stones of the same color are arranged at a right angle. It is known as a bad shape because it reduces efficiency and the chances of not being captured. The general practice was obviously to avoid bad shapes. But I didn't see it in that way. I believed that an empty triangle itself was inefficient, but could be the lifesaver depending on how the stones were laid out on the Go board.

At that first round of the semi-finals, I had an epiphany. What could potentially be a good empty triangle caught my eyes. I was convinced that what I was about to do was going to be a clever local move; to make a paired move above and below the empty triangle that would cut off my opponent's group of stones. Any professional Go player trained in Japan to play by the set shapes and principles would not have chosen to place the stone there. But, I did not care about shapes nor rules. I only wanted to win so I dared myself to make the move.

That day, experts on Go spoke about the "beginning of the Korean approach," which I deeply appreciated. It meant that Korean Go started to take its own course, breaking away from the standards established by the Japanese Go. Ever since that round, Korean Go did grow and prosper by breaking one by one the rules and the taboos defined by the players in Japan. Korean players began to play differently when they started to think differently. It got them as far as playing at a higher level than the Japanese Go players, the former world champions.

The Korean pattern, which the Japanese players have begun to notice, is different from the Japanese pattern in many ways. The Japanese pattern looks elegant with shapes forming simple lines. On the other hand, the Korean pattern looks bizarre. The shape cannot be called a pattern by any means. In the beginning, Japanese players scoffed at it for lacking sophistication, but they began to panic when the Korean pattern took them down too many times to call their defeats coincidences.

Korean players have even invented new way-outs the Japanese pattern never had. This achievement has brought tremendous shift in paradigm in the Go world. Japan has always pursued aesthetics in Go and its leadership in international Go meant everybody else accepted their way. The game of Go was about training oneself for self-discovery and enlightenment, and observing code of behavior and courtesy for good play. Then, the Korean Go came along, challenging to put all patterns and courtesies aside. Since then, Go began to be perceived as a competitive brain sport. A strong instinct for survival and the thirst for victory engendered an inventive way of thinking.

Who changes the world and makes history? History has shown us over and over that it's those who question the status quo and make the fierce attempt to fix the problem. Likewise, Go survived 4,000 years during which patterns have been continuously developed and discovered. It would not have made this far if it were not for the players who wanted to find out the 'why's and the 'how's of the established patterns.

Don't be afraid of thinking differently and applying them in real life. No matter how small it may seem, it can playout in so many different ways- may it be a small change in one's personal life, or a change for the better for everyone in this world.

THE CAGE-FREE SWALLOW

Every player has a different ethos, which shows during a match. Their personalities and mind set determine the tone of their moves and the flow of the match.

I have been told that I play like a swallow performing an airshow: tactical, unexpected aerobatic maneuvers with speed. My style has earned me the nickname, 'swallow Cho.' My only student, Lee Changho, is a

'Stone Buddha,' because he is steady and unflinching, even at his opponent's provocative moves. Among other top players in Korea, Seo Bong-soo is known as the 'weed' for his wild play; he doesn't mind getting into a 'mud fight' on the board. Yoo Changhyuk is deemed to execute the best 'colorful offense' in the world. Every successful professional Go player has a distinctive style and approach.

How a player chooses to see the world is what determines the style and approach of the play. It is also how they choose to live in the real world. So a match between two rivals is a clash of two different sets values. In this sense, Go is more than a game; it epitomizes the player's perspective on life and philosophy. This is precisely why after being around for 4 thousand years, it continues to be a popular game played both on and off-line.

Unfortunately, the creative potential of Go doesn't seem to be able to keep up with its popularity. Go styles have become so homogenous that a player with a distinctive approach is hard to find. I have to admit that nowadays, rookies have very strong foundation in Go and they play very well. But, wait a minute. Their styles ring a bell. I have seen someone else play like them before. I could not help but feel they were emulating veteran players, or were following the pattern others had created. At around mid-game, when the momentum is there and the spectators have been waiting long enough for a jaw-dropping move that could either make or break the game, the anticipation is quickly disappointed by a normal, obvious move. Go fans have started to complain that the game has become unexciting. What happened?

According to my observation, much has to do with how Go is taught in Korea nowadays. Children go to private Go classes after school to learn how to play in a short period of time. The teacher spoon-feeds the rules and the formulas and the students are expected to learn them by heart. The goal is to make them play the game and to please their parents with quick results. Go programs are structured in such a way that they leave very little room and time for children to think about the next move on their own, and deprives them of the freedom to imagine a new move. They are expected to place stones according to the formula they have memorized, which turns their match into a test to see who digested the most information, instead of a battle of ideas.

Training students in this way is only one of many conditions unfavorable for nurturing creative problem-solvers in Go. One can hardly expect anyone with a unique approach to come out of it. Students maybe trained for multiple choice questions, but never for essay questions. Learning to merely reproduce knowledge and skills is akin to molding machines programmed to produce individuals who think alike, at the expense of nurturing individuality. I find it very disturbing that most Go programs in Korea for young players are skewed to short-term goals.

One of the best things that happened to me was that I met a mentor, Kensaku Segoe, who encouraged me to be in close contact with my 'self.' Although not well known in Korea, Kensaku Segoe is a hero in Japan, revered as a founding father of the modern Japanese Go. All his life, he took in only three students; Go Seigen, a Chinese-born praised for changing the course of international Go; Utaro Hashimoto, who founded one of the two major Go associations in Japan, Kansai Ki-in that is headquartered in Osaka, and me.

Go Seigen is held in great respect as a 'Go Saint,' which is the title given to the winner of Kisei Title Match in Japan, but also an honorific expression used to address a player who has unmatched game skills. Go Seigen was praised for defeating all of his close rivals in a series of Juban-go, or a high-profile 'death match.' In a Jubango, whoever loses by four rounds is to bear the humiliation of getting an advantage in the next game while a handicap is given to the winner to make up for the difference in the level of the skills. None of Go Seigen's rivals walked out of the Juban-go without being mortified. Utaro Hashimoto was admired for sweeping the titles of well-established matches in Japan for over 3 decades, from the 1940s to 1970s. He won the titles of the Honinbo Title Match, the Oza Title Match, the Judan Title Match, and the Kisei Title Match as many as 9 times. 'Honinbo' is the leading Go house in Japan, and 'Judan (10P)' is an honorific title given to the winner, as the highest rank in profession-al Go game goes up to 9P only. Therefore, winning these two titles, in particular, was a reflection of Utaro Hashimoto's undisputed reputation. As for me, I became the winner of the first Ing Cup. All three of us who studied under Kensaku Segoe, did very well for ourselves in international matches, and we are very grateful to our mentor for everything he did, or did not do for us.

I was the last student Master Segoe took in to learn Go while living in his residence. My mentor was in his 80s and I was only eleven when I went to live with him. Master Segoe, Mama zzang, his daughter-in-law, myself, and Benkei, the dog, the four of us lived in a cozy Japanese style timber house. Master Segoe was sparing in his teaching. He hardly made himself available for lessons so much so that I could actually count the number of times we sat face-to-face for a game during the 9 years I lived with him. He was also very reserved, talking to me only to ask me to review the game I had played before.

I was apprehensive, confused and disappointed. Has he completely forgotten about me? Is he going senile? But, I was completely wrong about him.

One day, during dinner, Master Segoe gave me a hard stare and broke the silence. "Do you expect me to give you the answers? There are no such things as answer keys in Go. How can I give you what even I don't have? You should find the answers by yourself. That's how it is with Go." He added, "Go is all about making a ceaseless effort to find the answers even if there is no right or wrong answer."

Master Segoe never once said a single word about how I played. He had full knowledge of my practice partners and opponents, yet he never intervened. I enjoyed complete autonomy over how and what to work on under Master Segoe.

Giving the answer to a student who is lost is easy. But that student will never learn because the answer was given, not earned through hard work.

Master Kensaku Segoe knew exactly how to teach, or not teach, Go. He gave a broad direction and the rest of laissez-faire. Thanks to his educational philosophy, in my teens, I used to stay up all night just to figure out a single move that would solve the entire puzzle. It was not easy, but it was one of the best times of my life.

Anybody who has memorized the formulas can solve the questions. But they will realize that they are not prepared when they are given questions that are not straight forward. On the other hand, those who have spent a lot of time trying to figure out the answer on their own without the help of the answer keys, will be prepared to take on mind-stretching problems.

I never had formal training in Go. Such shortcoming allowed me to follow my heart and trust my way. All in all, it culminated into my own style, earning me a series of interesting nicknames, such as 'swallow Cho,' 'magician Cho,' and 'Cho, the flame thrower.'

The ability to think is a tool that leads one to the answers. It is what makes an individual's 'core self' strong. I believe that a truly happy individual is someone who has a strong 'core self.' Money, reputation, or success cannot make an individual truly happy. Those with a strong 'core self' are not swayed by people or events around them. They are not intimidated by how other people see them, or unreasonable social standards, but have the confidence to be themselves and go their way.

So set aside the time and space for the freedom to think.

CURIOUS RUI AND
THE KOBAYASHI PATTERN

"How do you come up with a new move?"

Ask any Go player and they will give the same reply; it's a discovery at the end of a tenacious wrestle with a problem. It is never planned or intended, but hours of grappling with the problem culminates in an Eureka moment. Having been trained for years, professional Go players know that the only way to come up with the next powerful move before the 10-second overtime count is over is to keep thinking until they get that flash of insight.

That is why I believe creativity is the result of resolute determination and persistent effort to search for solutions. The main ingredient for creativity is an enquiring mind, not intelligence.

A creative mind is not an exclusive property of a few geniuses in the world of arts and music or famous innovators in the tech community, such as Bill Gates or Steve Jobs. Everything and anything we do in our daily life can use some creativity. Sometimes one can be surrounded by ingenuity and not realize it.

My wife, Mihwa, is an amazing cook. Mihwa picks healthy ingredients that are cooked in ways that can be easily digested, but she also remembers to cook with the perfect seasoning-her own- to please the taste buds. Guests who have joined us for Mihwa's home-cooked meals have always been amazed at her healthy dishes that came with a pleasant delicious twist of their own. They have always asked her for the recipe. Being a modest woman, Mihwa has always accepted their request to be a formal courteous way of appreciating her effort until a publisher asked her if she was interested in writing a cook book.

I believe that ingenuity in a broad sense is an 'idea that other people cannot imagine.' Ideas do not just spring up. They are earned by the inquisitive mind who goes through the arduous process of asking why and how. One who desires to understand and learn asks a series of questions; why did it happen? What went wrong? What can be done differently to make it better? Did we do our best? The mind has to be curious and willing to go through trials-and-error until the expected outcome is achieved to its satisfaction. Mihwa wanted to cook her family nutritious but tasty meals so she experimented with her recipes until she found the gold standard that worked for her. What was a journey of discovery for her was deemed as natural creativity by others.

Creativity stems from the unwillingness to wait for answers. Impatience and excitement combine to force oneself to think out of the box and seek for the answers.

Professional Go masters are a group of people who cannot stand if a problem remains unsolved, especially, if it is about Go. When we come across an amusingly unfamiliar move that we cannot explain, we obsess over it while walking on the road, doing other businesses, and even in bed. We also run to our colleagues for a piece of advice because two brains at work is better than one after all.

Rui Naiwei was a Chinese-born professional Go player who played in Korea. In 1988, she became the first woman professional player in the world to be promoted to 9P. Rui's Go career was quite eventful contrary to her placid personality. In 1989, she was forced to leave China because of a disagreement with the Chinese Weiqi Association. Rui drifted back and forth between Japan and the U.S. for a decade unable to play any Go. It was only in 1999 that with the generous help of the Korea Baduk Association that Rui started to play Go again in Korea, where she dominated women's tournaments; Rui went from strength-to-strength, winning all-women's championships 26 times. The highlight of her 13-year achievement in Korea was winning the Guksu Title match, the oldest tournament in Korea which was always won by men. The year she became the champion of that match, Rui beat me. She became the first woman and a non-Korean 'Guksu,' meaning the National Hand, an honorific and affectionate title Korean give to the master of Go. She was a Go sensation.

One day, I ran into Rui in the Korea Baduk Association. She was excited and she showed me a picture. "What would be the next move when we change the order of the stones placed in this pattern here?"

That was 'Kobayashi pattern', a deviation from the standard pattern, named after Koichi Kobayashi who was fond of it during the 1980s when he was playing on top of everyone in Japan. The Kobayashi pattern was one of the time-tested widely accepted pattern. Nobody questions Kobayashi, except for Rui who seemed to be not quite satisfied with the pattern. She was suspecting that the pattern could become vulnerable from moving a single stone. I could not give an answer right away. A few days later, I brought it up when I met my Go friends. My student, Lee Changho, was also there. "Rui 9P thinks the Kobayashi pattern is vulnerable. What do you think? "I a...

We were all ... ...us and excited to talk about the question Rui has raised, even i... ...'t have a board or a piece of paper in front of us. At first, we th... ...e found a weak link in the Kobayashi pattern as Rui suspected. Ho... ...er, after an in-depth discussion, we concluded that what looked like a weak link did not have any impact on the entire flow of game. But, during our discussion, Changho discovered a new move that no one else did.

If Rui hadn't questioned the pattern, we would not have gone through the trouble of testing her suspicion, in turn, Changho would not have found a move which was new to all of us.

A professional Go player never assumes anything. There is a reason for every move made by the opponent. 'Why is the stone placed there?' 'What is the intention of the move?' We ask fiercely and force ourselves to think in a brutally short period of time before we decide on the next move.

Likewise, every move in real life must count like the stones in Go. One simply cannot excuse oneself from making choices based on hunches, social pressure, coercion, or time constraint.

Every question that pops into our mind must be dealt with seriously even if it cannot be answered right away. Why are things the way they are? How can issues and situations be fixed? What could be the most reasonable and efficient way to deal with them? These questions must be posed and answered.

Such system of inquiry, I believe, is applicable to every aspect of our life, whether it be for school, work, relationships, or self-management. Memorized information is volatile and short-term whereas the knowledge acquired through inquiry is stable and long-█ ██ █ ecomes a strong foundation that improves performance and dev█ ███ well-rounded personality. The answers to the inquiry may not alway█ ██ what is looked for. However, there is little to regret and more courage █ take responsibility of the choices one makes based on those self-earned answers.

When the question, 'why?' springs in the mind, is an opportunity to move forward. It is an opportunity not to be missed. One must think hard to answer the question. There is a reason for everything and there is always a better way to do things.

Thinking is not always exciting, more likely to give headaches. It can cause more confusion rather than giving straight answers. But the feeling of joy that is waiting at the other end of the tunnel is of something not to be traded with anything. The joy of enlightenment is overwhelming. When such inquiry-based approach in life becomes a habit, and not to mention, the more it is repeated the better we become at it and the faster we can get to the answers. Above all, it becomes a fortress that guards one against any troubles in life and gives the space to strategize and launch a counter-attack with confidence.

"Every move and choice reveals
one's values and how one sees the world."

Chapter 2

Good ideas Come from a Nice man

THE 600 YEN LESSON

I was within an inch of bidding an eternal farewell to Go when I was 15, while studying under Master Segoe. I was then a member of the Fujisawa study group, privately-run by Shuko Fujisawa who was famous for his eccentric and controversial behavior. I went down to Fujisawa almost every day to hang out and play a game or two with some of the best Go players in Japan of the time, including Hideo Otake, the professional Go player who ruled the Japanese Go community in the 1970s, and Rin Kaiho, the Taiwanese-born professional player who was also a top player in Japan from the late 1960s to the 1990s.

Master Fujisawa was the super star of all professional players in Japan. Master Segoe was looked upon like a grandfather figure because of his stern and intimidating style, while Master Fujisawa was admired like a friendly father figure. Whenever Master Fujisawa saw me, he would roll up his sleeves and play the buffoon before the young boy.

"Bring it on, Kunken!" He would challenge me, calling my name with Japanese accent.

We always played quick games. Master Fujisawa believed that Go should be played with intuition, or flashes of wit rather than calculated strategies. I was a player of that disposition. When we played against each other, the sound of the stones echoed like the clopping of shod hooves on the pavement, brisk but louder with each move.

In retrospect, I believe I found comfort at Fujisawa. I was lonely at Master Segoe's place where there was hardly anyone to speak to. At Fujisawa, not only did I play Go as much as I wanted in the company of other players, but I also found friendship even though I was the youngest. Most of the players who came to Fujisawa were grown-ups and they were generous to me. I felt welcomed and taken care of. Yoshiteru Abe, who was 6P, always asked me, a mere 2P, to play games with him. I always crushed him but he never stopped asking me to play.

One afternoon, Abe came up to me and asked to play, as always. "Kunken, let's play for some money today!"

No way. There were two things Master Segoe strictly forbade me from doing- gambling and playing Go for money. "I'm sorry but I can't. Master Segoe told me never to play games for money." But Abe would not give up. He insisted that I accept his offer. "It's o.k. when we are playing at Fujisawa. Come on, it's just you and me." "I'm really sorry but I have to reject your offer. Master Segoe said never." I felt sweat run down my neck as I was trying to politely turn down his request. Master Fujisawa, who was watching our scuffle nearby, threw in a helping word, "Kunken, you don't have to think of it as a gamble because you are betting just for fun.

48

Betting 100 yen per round is o.k."

I could not get myself out of it. So I sat down to play with Abe. All of the members at Fujisawa crowded around us and began to cheer. "Kunken, don't be too hard on him." "Abe, knock Kunken down to size!" By the time the sound of the cheer became deafening, I had forgotten about Master Segoe's words and I became obsessed with only one thing- I wanted to win.

Abe and I ended up playing three rounds. I won all three. I should have stopped right there but Abe, feeling sore and hot under the collar, insisted that we continue. So we did. The fourth round was quickly followed by the fifth and the sixth. Abe admitted his defeat after I won all six rounds in a row.

That day, I won 600 yen. I refused to receive the money, but Abe insisted on paying me to keep his word. He put the money into my hand. Days went by and I had completely forgotten about the incident until one day, Master Segoe called me. "Kunken, come over here."

Master Segoe had a stern look on his face. "Did you play Go for money with Yoshiteru Abe?" I knew that I had to admit it. When I said yes, his face turned scary. I had never seen such a frightening expression on his face before.

"Get out of my house right now! You don't deserve to learn Go. I sever the relationship I have had with you today. Go back to Korea!"

Master Segoe was a man of his word. Once he made a decision that was the end. He never accepted any excuses nor apologies. I packed some clothes and left his house. Mama zzang, his daughter-in-law, paced the floor anxiously, feeling sorry for me. She followed me to the front gate but was called back in by the furious roar of Master Segoe.

I thought I was having a blackout. A lot of people back in Korea had high expectations for me which was why I had come all the way to Japan to study Go. I could not believe I was being thrown out for something that I did not even initiate. What terrified me most was the culture of the Go community in Japan. Any player who has been expelled from one Go house does not get a second chance with any other Go houses. Once you are out, you are out. A scandal like this could destroy me forever. Even if I went back to Korea and kept playing Go, the dishonor will follow me to the grave.

I walked around aimlessly for a while. I had nowhere to go and no plans. I wandered through the streets of Tokyo until darkness began to fall. It was only then that I realized I had to bring my senses together and find a place to stay. The only place I could think of was a Korean restaurant run by a Korean expatriate where I was a regular. The owner took me in in exchange for helping with dish-washing and cleaning.

The following day, I began my work early in the morning and finished late at night. I washed and pruned the vegetables, washed the dishes, cleaned the floor and the kitchen. The first week went by and the second week had passed. I did not know whether it was time for me to leave Japan nor how to explain it to my parents. There was nothing I could do except to make a call to Mama zzang every night to ask if Master Segoe was still angry and if there was any chance for him to accept me again. I choked up every time I called her, in distress and regret.

About ten days later, Mama zzang had news for me. She said I could return because Master Segoe had worked off his fury. It sounded too good to be true. Is this really happening? Has a stubborn man like him really forgiven me and is willing to take me back? I ran to his house right away with half hope and half doubt. When I pressed the door bell, the gate opened. Master Segoe took one look at me and did not say anything. We had dinner together without speaking a word and each went back to our own rooms, as we usually did. He drank a cup of sake and I opened a Go book. Everything was the same as usual, as if nothing had ever happened.

Later, I learned that many people in the Go community who heard about how I got kicked out, paid a visit to Master Segoe to offer an explanation. Abe and even Master Fujisawa came by a few times to ask for forgiveness on my behalf. Abe, in particularly, blamed himself for getting me into trouble. He felt guilty for insisting to bet money on the game and for telling the whole town about it. Abe confessed that his intention was to commend my talent, never to get me into trouble. Abe had no idea Master Segoe would be as furious as to punish me for it.

This incident became a complete nightmare for me. No matter how many times I revisited the day I played the game for money, I could not come up with any way to reject Abe's request. I would have done the same thing even if I went back in time to that moment.

But the fact was that I had broken the rule Master Segoe had been adamant about. Regardless of the context, I broke the rule and deserved to take responsibility for the consequence. Master Segoe's rule was too unreasonable and his reaction too terrifying for a 15-year-old boy to comprehend and handle. It took me years to slowly process and understand Master Segoe. By then I had become an adult, had taken in a student myself and had enough life experiences to fully appreciate Master Segoe's teaching.

I believe Master Segoe recognized that my talent would make me a great Go player in the world on the first day we met. But he was not sure if I had the character to win. Will he grow into a good person with the character that befits his talent in Go? Long before I went into tutelage under Master Segoe, he had already decided not to take in any more students. But he made the exception of accepting me, at a very old age, because he felt a sense of mandate to help me win with talent and character- become a true master in Go.

As the saying goes, you never offer a high position or the secret of a special technique to those who have questionable personality, and never put skills and knowledge before virtue. Master Segoe warned me over and over about betting money on Go, even for a mere few hundred yen, he knew that if I did not take his words seriously, I would end up with fatal flaws in my character later in life.

If Master Segoe had not punished me the way he had, I would never have developed a sense of guilt about straying into sideways occasionally. I could have become indifferent to bending rules and too comfortable with "ends justifies the means" way of thinking. Several times in my life, I did come very close to making compromises that would endanger my reputation and values. I am only human with many shortcomings after all. But it was the teachings of Master Segoe that helped me get a hold on myself. I resisted the temptation of easy life and stopped myself from crossing the line. I never stopped thinking about the virtues of a good Go player.

THINK RIGHT, ACT RIGHT

From time to time, people of great wealth and high-ranking in business or in the government, find themselves mired in scandals for inappropriate comments or behavior in public; anything from human mistakes, such as a careless body language, slip of the tongue to the more controversial, professional and moral misconduct, accounting frauds, and backdoor dealings. Shouldn't the wealthy and the elite know better than to get themselves involved in wrongdoings?

Rule-breaking or socially-misbehaving people are often the ones who are in the limelight- on fast track to success and this creates great confusion. Did breaking the rules get them that far? Do I need to start bending the rules myself to become successful? Will I end up with the short end of the stick if I continue complying to the rules and moral ethics? Our values are shaken by the few powerful and wealthy people who do not appear to deserve their success. But time always reveals that their success is only an illusion, a house of cards soon to collapse. They may appear to be on a roll, but their tricks and deceptions do come with a hefty price tag later.

In the world of Go, although very rarely, one comes across some professional players who resorts to cheap tricks rather than playing fair and square. For example, they induce their opponents to inadvertently break petty rules, such as the rule related to using the timer or placing the stones on the board. At first look, the loss or the discredit seems to make sense because however minor, the player broke the rule. But a closer look always reveals that the player had fallen for a sneaky ambush attack. When it happened to me, I was furious and thought it was an unfair way to lose. But I did not do anything about it because I knew that those who use unethical tactics do not last long. Cheating can earn one a victory or two, but it does not translate into one's real performance. One will never make it to the top of the world from using dishonest practices.

Not everyone can make it to the top. Hard work nor skills alone can't guarantee a place in the summit. One needs the complete package that includes character and luck. Above all, a player must have a strong core, or the mental strength to bear the pressure of playing with the best players. The skills will take the player to the top, but to stay on the top, one needs the character to bear the weight of the crown.

Having the character does not always translate into better performance right away. In order to seek immediate gains, one should make practical use of time. But the moment when one's character is put the test may come sooner than expected. Character is revealed in one's every word, gesture, and behavior, therefore, it becomes the yardstick of one's reputation. One's reputation is established before one realizes it.

A crisis situation brings out one's true character. Does one eat humble pie, or shift the blame on others to protect self-interest? How does one use power and for what cause? One's choices define what one stands for. Character allows one to use intelligence and talent in the right way. Without the befitting character, one is bound to think in ill-disciplined ways and make destructive decisions. Without righteous mind one is unable to choose the right thing to do, chances are one ends up with facing ruins.

So it is crucial to train oneself to think right. One's choices and actions are reflection of how one thinks. To get a better idea of a person, pay attention to the choices that person makes instead of what is spoken. A single decision will give a more accurate picture than a thousand words.

History has taught us the same; Adolf Hitler was a genius but his obsession with eugenics and imperialism was a deadly threat to humanity. Joseph V. Stalin, blinded by the desire for power, conceived his version of the Reign of Terror and ruthlessly eliminated his political rivals.

One's thoughts grow like a tree, branching out in the direction of the sun. But one wrong turn can forever change the course of the branch. I believe rules and the moral code, no matter how trivial they may seem, must be internalized every day, so that they make up the strong foundation of one's character to think right and act right.

SHADOWING MY MASTER

Master Segoe took me in as his last student to mold my character around the virtues desirable for both Go and life. Master Segoe, however, did not micromanage what I did, or did not do. Except for setting a few basic ground rules that included prohibiting gambling and playing Go for money, he did not keep a list of do's and don'ts. He never gave me a lecture on what kind of person I should be. Instead, Master Segoe led by example.

Master Segoe had a regimented daily routine; he got up every day at the same time, got dressed and read the newspaper. After having a light breakfast, he spent all day thinking about Go or reading books. In between, he took slow walks in the front yard. Whenever he had guests over, Master Segoe did not make a fuss to welcome them. He seemed uninterested in the politicians and ministers who paid him visits. Once, a homeless came by asking for food. Master Segoe treated him with the same indifference he had shown to his high-ranking guests.

The only guest who was welcomed at Master Segoe's house was Yasunari Kawabata, his long-time friend and the author of "Snow Country (Yukiguni)" who won the Nobel Prize for Literature in 1968.

Whenever Mr. Kawabata came over, the two gentlemen caught up with each other, but mainly talked about Go and literature while sipping their tea. They spoke so softly in a low voice that I could hardly hear what they were talking about.

In the evening, Master Segoe liked to sip sake very slowly while having dinner. He loved sake very much. Considering his old age and his health, which was not in a good shape after being exposed to the radiation from the atomic bombs that dropped in Hiroshima, it was probably better for Master Segoe to quit drinking any alcohol. But Master Segoe never gave up his love for sake. His doctor begged him to stop drinking but he always shook his head sideways saying, "please do not ask me to give up sake even if it kills me tomorrow."

The doctor limited the amount of sake Master Segoe could drink in a day to one hop, about 180ml. He also made Master Segoe promise to drink a cup of sake slowly for over one or two hours, and never to imbibe. Master Segoe gave his word to the concerned doctor and kept his promise until the day he died. I liked watching my mentor in his kimono sipping sake at the dinner table without saying a word. He took one grateful sip at a time, inhaling its fragrance, too. He looked like a man meditating in a scroll of a Japanese painting.

His way of life was admirable but perhaps too monotonous for someone outgoing and curious like me. I could not have stood the strictly regimented daily routine. Master Segoe devoted his entire life to Go and did not bother to learn much about the real world. Naturally, he was clueless when it came to the price of daily necessities, for example, the price of a pen or a bale of rice so he often paid through the nose. But he chose to live in solitude, religiously devoting himself to Go. As for me, I knew that I did not want to live like a Go hermit, let alone have the capacity to follow in the footsteps of my master.

I did not want to let Go govern my whole life. Even the 'expulsion' episode did not stop me from being curious about the world outside Go. For example, there were so many fascinating games like pachinko in Japan, mah-jong in China, and poker in the Western world. I wanted to explore those seemingly challenging and entertaining territories myself. Master Segoe's way of life was akin to a still-life painting, which would have made me feel out of breath if I were to emulate it. I had a lot of respect for my master but at times I found his views to be somewhat out of date and too conservative for the 20th century.

Go was my passion but I never came close to feeling a sense of spiritual responsibility for it like Master Segoe did. There have been too many interesting things happening outside the Go world that I just had to try. If Master Segoe was alive, I am afraid he would have wanted to sever ties with me for having an affair behind Go; I have seen the world, gambled with cards, and betted on horse racing.

I lived with Master Segoe for 9 years. During this time, whether it be Go or his view of the world, he taught me by setting an example. We were two different people with different dispositions and we went our own ways. Now that I have arrived at his age I realized that we had a common ground; we both loved Go and led lives that revolved around it.

While I was studying under Master Segoe, he was always there for me and I grew up watching him; I saw the way he treated others, the way he played Go with integrity, the way he was always neatly and properly dressed, and carrying on his daily routine like a ritual. The underlying meaning of his words that I once unjustly brushed off became clearer as I got older.

"The most important thing in life is to do our duty as a human being."

"Integrity, character, and dignity are what make us a complete human being."

"The duty of a teacher is not to give the answers, but to show the way and to give support."

Manners can be taught but integrity and character cannot. Attempting to mold the character of an individual itself risks ruining the true character of that person. Master Segoe showed me his way hoping that I would learn from his example instead of rolling his sleeves up to educate me.

There is no need to scold the students for falling short of one's standards and expectations. As long as one holds fast to one's principles, those inspired will work hard to follow the example of the teacher. Those who choose otherwise do so most probably because the values and the principles considered important in the teacher's days may have become less important today.

For those of us who are worried about kids who do not behave, there is no magic spell to discipline them. Stop looking for tricks. Rather, set a good example. Children imitate the grown-ups. They are our mirrors. It is highly likely that children who get distracted easily and are clumsy grow up under parents who more or less have difficulty concentrating.

Poor parents are those who have very little principles and values to teach their children, not those who have little money to give. Children's lives depend on the values and perspectives they learn from their parents because they form the foundation of their social skills, career choices, raising a family and pursuing their dreams.

BEARING THE WEIGHT OF THE CROWN

In 1989, when I came home from the Ing Cup with the champion's trophy, Lee Changho, my student, bowed with no facial expression like the statue of the Buddha. He did not say a single word of congratulations nor gave me a smile. As soon as I arrived at the Gimpo Airport, Korea, I was whisked away in a motorcade through the streets of Seoul to downtown while crowds greeting me in a festive mood. I also received hundreds of phone calls from the Go community congratulating me. But, as it was always the case, I did not get any special reaction from my own student. Changho and I were both the reserved kind. Instead of giving me a rowdy praise, Changho hung around in the living room for a while and tried to read my face, which I knew, was his way of congratulating me. And then he retired to his room.

Changho passed the Professional Qualification Tournament two years after he came to learn under my tutelage. He was a fast learner and came home with dozens of trophies every time he participated in a tournament. But never once did I offer him a congratulatory word nor did Changho express his excitement. On the other hand, Mihwa would grab both of Changho's hands and give him a big hug to show how happy she was for him. Changho would then, show a brief, faint smile to reciprocate. Changho and I never exchanged any compliments, nor offered any words of comfort when one of us was defeated. We just stared into space without saying a word. What an uninteresting relationship!

I took in Changho as my student in 1984, when I was 31. It was very rare at the time for an active professional Go player, who was still in his prime time, to accept a student. I did not plan on it myself as I had always thought if I ever took in a student, the right time would be after retirement.

Changho was a boy of few words but became even quieter like a stone Buddha after he started to live with us. Not only did he speak less and less, but his facial expressions disappeared, and he even acted like an old man. A nine-year old boy walked trying hard not to make any noise as if he wanted to be invisible. Mihwa, who looked after him, took pity on him. Changho had left his parents too young to live with complete strangers. Mihwa thought he did not feel home at our place. I understood very well how Changho must have felt, to be away from home and having to mingle with grown-ups at that age. He must have felt lonely and uncomfortable. But it was the price he had to pay to learn Go. He had to force himself to become mature to compete with grown-ups. So I spared friendliness, warmth and kindness.

Winning and losing is as natural as eating a meal to a professional Go player. Having meal is not a special one-day event. It is a routine that must continue until we die. There is no need to be excited for the delicious food today, or be disappointed by an awful one the next day. If one fails to learn how to control one's emotions, one will not last in the world of professional competition. Don't be overjoyed by one victory nor get upset too much about one defeat. Training to control emotions no matter under what circumstances precedes perfecting skills. Only those who can keep calm get to climb to the summit.

Master Segoe never scolded me when I lost, nor spoke highly of me when I won. Every day was the same to him- whether I was biting my tongue, unable to get over a stupid mistake that eventually led to my defeat, or whether I was thrilled from winning a landslide victory. Master Segoe always had me do those tedious chores like sweeping the yard clean or preparing a table of sake and snacks. He trained me to embrace joy and woe like a daily routine so that I would not be swayed by emotions. Emotions are merely waves that get washed away to the sea or washed up to the shore. Master Segoe believed that one should never be consumed by emotions. Professional Go players, in particular, were to detach themselves from joy, sorry, and anger and process them with a cool head. Master Segoe warned that those used to feeling flattered from winning are not able to bear being defeated. In order to win, one must have the experience of losing one thousand times until one becomes strong enough to treat victory and defeat as business-as-usual. I grew up watching and learning from Master Segoe how to never lose control of emotions.

It is easier said than done, of course. It is hard even for professional

Go players to accept defeat with grace. They may choose to turn to their families for consolation and comfort. But it was not the case for me. Rain or shine, I went to bed as usual and got up the next morning at the same time. It was not easy to be in control of my emotions. Sometimes, I would toss and turn, failing to shake off the misery of defeat. Then I would get out of the bed to take a slow walk in the front yard or try to read a book until the feeling of anger or resentment gradually subsides.

I did not teach Changho how to play Go. The only thing I could do for him was to be myself, just like Master Segoe did for me. If Changho thought I had any strengths, it was really up to him to embrace it. As for my weaknesses, I believe he had the capacity to ignore them. It was his judgement call.

Changho may have been disappointed about being the only live-in student as well as not getting any one-on-one structured lessons from me. He must have had high expectations when he decided to learn Go from someone deemed to be one of the best in the world. But I was very pleased to see how Changho turned out the way I hoped he would. He was diligent and devoted to learning Go. He grew into a man of few words who was never swayed by anything like the stone Buddha. Today, Changho lives a peaceful life, carries out his duties with a strong sense of responsibility, and is never involved in any scandalous event. Therefore, I feel it is fair to say that I have done everything I could for him.

In the final game of the 29th Choegowi Title Match, which is one of the prestigious and the second-oldest title matches in Korea where I had won 15 times, Changho sat opposite me after fearlessly beating every great master of the time. Changho and I had actually played against each other- 'mentor vs mentee'- twice, in 1988 and 1989. But this time something was different. Changho was the sun, rising with great energy, and I felt the heat taking over me. I fought hard to make a two-to-two draw, but I lost in the final round by half a point.

That night, Changho and I came home in the same car. We put my family in an awkward position. They could not congratulate Changho nor say something nice to me. Whatever our innermost feelings were, we acted as usual. I went straight to bed and Changho spent an hour or two practicing Go before he went to bed. But it was a day to remember for both of us; to Changho, it must have been the best day of his life. To me, it was both a cruel and happy day. And yet, we went about our business as usual.

STEPPING DOWN FROM THE THRONE

Changho winning the championship of the Choegowi Title Match was a sensation. The fact that a 15-year-old boy rose to the thrown by beating his own mentor who was still looking after him made headlines. It was an unprecedented event in the history of Go in Korea.

Usually, the age difference between a teacher and the students in Go community is huge. The reason is because most professional players accept student later in their career, and the incubation time for students is long. Seeing a teacher and a student playing against each other is very rare. Even I expected to play against Changho in my mid-forties, at the earliest. But Changho grew at a fast pace beyond my expectation. I was at my best when I lost my Choegowi championship title to Changho in 1990. I was 37. I was more surprised than pleased at the sudden success of my own student.

And it did not stop there. Changho and I played against each other again at the Guksu Title Match in September 1990. This time, he beat me three to nothing. Changho went from strength to strength, winning the Daewang Title Match, the Wangwi Title Match, and the Myeongin Title Match. He took away all three titles from me, one by one. By the end of 1991, Changho had won seven different championship titles while I was left with only 4. Changho moved out around this time to live on his own. Even for us poker-faces, it was awkward to be in the same space, especially after we had played against each other. Besides, Changho had outgrown me. He had learned everything and I had nothing more to teach.

Changho and I let the events of our lives take their own course. The day he moved out, he bowed without any expression, just like the day he came to live with us. Mihwa tried very hard to hold back her tears and I, I gazed after him without saying a word. After he became independent, Changho's attack gathered even more force, and I was freefalling straight down. Playing against Changho left me exhausted. Back then, each player was given five hours so the games continued past 10 p.m. I became aware of the limit of my physical strength. I felt as if my body was breaking into pieces when I was using up all energy to calculate every possible effective move. At one point, I had to almost lie down during a game with him even when the cameras were there. The media described it as, "the Master reclined elegantly to play some Go," which was a nice way to put it. But nothing could have been more humiliating for a middle-aged emperor of Go to be pulled down from his throne by some 16-year-old boy.

I had lost almost all of my titles to Changho. But Changho went on to target the only title I had been left with. In February of 1995, Changho took away the remaining last title from me. For the first time in my 20-year career, I was empty handed. I had no crowns left.

But strange enough, I felt a sense of tranquility when I returned home. I had lost everything, but I felt free and relieved. For the next few days, I caught up on my sleep and got a good rest. I felt better, physically and mentally. It felt like a new beginning. I started to have positive thoughts. Being without a title meant I had nothing to lose. I had put every ounce of my energy to defend the championship titles I had held, but once I've lost everything, I was surprised to find myself feel a great sense of freedom. Now that I had fallen to the bottom, it could not get any worse. Up was the only way to go. All I needed was to make one small step forward to call it a progress.

In retrospect, I was desperate to keep my head above water. Otherwise, the agony and excruciating pain would have consumed me. And then there was my love for Go. I could never quit Go. I had to play Go to live. For all of these reasons, I had to think positive and it got me through the cruelest time of my life.

Despair is difficult to overcome. Sometimes the feeling of loss is so deep that it completely demotivates us, forcing us to live in seclusion, or take our own lives. Fortunately, I realized I had the strength to laugh off at a crisis- a strength possibly inherited from my parents or a legacy of Master Segoe. Or, the strength could have stemmed from the unwavering support and confidence my family has always given me. Without them, I would not have lived through the tough time, or be called 'Cho, the Go Emperor.' Positive thinking also renewed my gratitude to everyone who took care of me and loved me.

Slowly but steadily, I climbed my way up from the dark abyss to the surface. I participated in almost every competition, playing games more than anyone else. I played 110 games in 1996 alone, which means I had a game every three days. I was no longer defending my championship title, but had to win all the way up to get to the finals. Losing one round meant falling straight down, which ironically made the game more thrilling. It was also refreshing to compete with young rookies after a long time.

I had always thought I was used to winning and losing all those years. But I was completely wrong about myself; I was used to winning but not losing. It was around this time that I began to care less about winning. I have come to accept that I was not always meant to win. As I felt more comfortable with myself, I began to smile more and joke with younger players. I even made a big fuss about being attacked, asking them to go easy on me.

Changho had become the winner who took it all, while I kept climbing up to make as many opportunities as I could to challenge him. We met again at the Guksu Title Match in 1998. Changho, as the defending champion, and I as the contender. I did my best to push him to surrender at the 159th move. But it was not about beating him. What was important to me was that I was able to work my way up to the top again. I also understood that even if I succeed in arriving at the summit, there were new rising stars other than Changho, who could push me off the top. But I wanted to prove myself and others that I was not easy.

I happened to read Changho's interview when he had lost all of his titles in 2011. When asked how he felt, Changho said, "Once I was defeated, I found myself at ease. I am not too hung up on the fact that I do not have any titles left. As long as I can play good games, I believe I can always get good results."

I smiled at his reply. I believe Changho finally understood how I felt. To empty the mind and to enjoy playing Go.

"Never give up too early.

I held on until I reached the next round of the game and the next…

not because I was craving to win,

but because there was light at the end of tunnel."

Chapter 3

Win,
if You Can

THE WAITING GAME

In 1997, in the final first round of the 8th Tongyang Securities Cup, an international professional Go championship, I faced my opponent, Satoru Kobayashi 9P who had defeated Lee Changho at the semi-final. Kobayashi was a placid tempered player who dominated the Japanese Go in the 1980s. The game was not going in my favor; my stone group had collapsed too early into the game because of a single careless misreading of a move. Ever since then, Kobayashi was coming after me. It was obvious that Kobayashi was very close to winning the game and all there was left for me to do seemed to accept my defeat.

But the tide started to change. I launched last-ditch attacks to win back control of the game. I knew I was stretching backward but noticed that Kobayashi was losing his pace. Kobayashi was agitated and began to overreact to my equally irrational moves. He could have just easily blocked my stones by simply removing them out of his way as he did before. But he did not. Did his obsession with winning blind him from thinking clearly? It occurred to me then that there might be a silver lining after all.

The game was not over yet. There were many minutes left before the empty spaces could be filled with stones. I was not going to let him have his way; I provoked him incessantly. Those who were watching the game live on the T.V. must have thought I was pathetic, trying to grasp on to the slightest chance to survive.

Finally, the chance that I had been waiting for while I doggedly held out had come. Kobayashi put his stone at the wrong place. I think he was confused. That move completely turned around the game like a flash. Kobayashi began to lose control at my vehement attack. The game ended at the 230th move. When the scores were counted, I beat him by six and half points.

"Cho Hunhyun went too far."

Observers clicked their tongue after the game. The atmosphere in the room was disapproving of my victory as they thought I had clung on to Kobayashi like a leech to deliberately trip him up. Kobayashi was in disbelief, sitting there with a blank expression. He was stunned in silence after losing the game he had almost won.

A few days later, Kobayashi and I sat across each other for the second round. And once again, I was cornered by Kobayashi's impeccable strategy. The stone group that I had laid out in the middle of the board was facing a virtual wipeout. It was obvious that I was trailing badly and almost losing the second round by half-time. But then, another unexpected development took place. While we were engaged in a Ko fight, where the white and the black stone takes turn to capture and recapture each other, Kobayashi made a Ko threat that was not really a threat.

When I realized what Kobayashi had done, I knew how I wanted to respond. I removed Kobayashi's black stone which stood in the way of my group. My group, which had been cut in half, was now perfectly connected, and the game turned into my favor in the blink of an eye. Once again, I won by one point.

The third round played out in the similar way. Halfway through the game, I had barely built my own territory except for some at the lower right corner while Kobayashi was trailblazing through the stones and expanding his territory. Everyone was expecting Kobayashi to win this time because he had lost by a neck after almost winning the previous two rounds. But, once again, a golden opportunity arose. A move that I had experimented with towards the end of the game turned out to work out beautifully and became the game-deciding one-side Ko. A one-side Ko, also known as a picnic Ko, is not a fatal blow to the one who is defeated; but the other player must win at all costs to avoid catastrophic damage. Kobayashi placed his stones on the board to resign at the 285th move.

It was a much-needed triumph, my first trophy at an international competition since I last won anything, locally or internationally. For the past two years and eight months, I was unable to pull myself out of a slump, especially, in local competitions.

This particular game is still the talk of the town. Kobayashi was prevailing in all three rounds until I bit him like a German Shepherd and did not let go until he kneeled down. I earned the reputation of being worse than death.

But that is just how it goes in the world of competition, as well as in the real world. The end result is as important as the process. We must win, if we can. And in order to win, one must hang on long enough for the right timing to launch a counter-attack.

When I was playing against Kobayashi in the Tongyang Securities Cup, I held out in the final three rounds because I believed I stood a chance to win the game. There was hope for me. It is different from being driven by acquisitiveness. I believe that a true fighter has the audacity to bet even on the slimmest chance to win when the game is not over. If I had chosen to admit defeat looming at the end of the game and thrown my stones to resign, would I have lasted long enough to have that opportunity to see the game turn for the better?

In a marathon, hundreds of runners start at the same time, but only one gets to cut the finishing tape. The rest of the marathoners know that there can be only one winner, and that they are not the one. Nevertheless, they keep running to cross that finishing line. Not a single runner stops running in the middle of the race or stops caring about the race just because the winner was already decided. Why? It is because there are other runners to outrun. But more importantly, it is for personal-best time that they keep running.

I believe that was exactly what a Go champion and a true fighter like Kobayashi was doing playing against me. Kobayashi fully admitted his defeat at the awards ceremony. "Whoever wins in the end is the stronger of the two, regardless of whether it was a good game throughout or not. The loser has nothing to say."

Professional Go is a game of mind-control. The moment one chooses to give up, the game is really over. On the other hand, if one believes that there is still hope to turn the tables around and looks for the right timing to make the move, the opportunity will present itself. Win the game, if at all possible. Never give up so easily. Put up a fight to the end. There is always a next time to reverse the tide.

MARKING TERRITORIES

The game of Go, simply put, is all about expanding into more territories than the opponent. The aim is to put as many black or white stones as possible, to capture the opponent's stones, 'build' houses and surround more territory. As such, defending one's own territory and conquering the opponent's territory becomes the life goal of a professional Go player. From the moment I grasped the stone for the first time in my life I have always given my best to expand my turf.

Expanding territory is a common goal in many different types of sports. American football, for example, is a game of advancing into the opponent's territory by throwing the ball to the other side. The offense is to run as hard as possible to advance the ball down the field. A successful catch that makes it to the touchdown, or kicked through the air for a field goal, means the offense has succeeded in penetrating into the defense side of the field. It is the same for handball and basketball. The ball is dribbled or passed down to the opponent's side of the court to be thrown at the goal. In soccer, the only difference would be the ball has to be controlled by feet. As such, in order to invade into the opponent's territory to score a goal, players end up struggling together on the field. The play can get very tense and tight with players giving it their all.

The goal of expanding territory and the fierce nature of this objective are very much part of the real everyday life. Everyone aims to win. They are willing to take great pains to have a better life, to get to a higher position, to live in a bigger house, and to drive a bigger car. We are all driven by our own ambitions which is perfectly natural. It can work as a healthy motivational mechanism as long as the reward is not acquired by illegal or inappropriate means, or comes at someone else's expense.

When I was young, I was brimming with the fighting spirit. I was obsessed with winning. I was possessed with the desire to win, so much so that every day and night was spent reading through books about game records. I was thinking about Go all the time. I endured years of harsh training in a foreign land because I wanted to win so badly.

Every Go player I knew in Japan was a genius. There were so many of them. Yoshio Ishida and Masao Kato, the two comets of the Japanese Go community of the 1970s; Koichi Kobayashi; and Cho Chikun. I played against many of them who had gone down the history of international Go as best of the best. In first few years, I got clobbered, barely surviving when I played against them. I had been acclaimed as a child prodigy when I became the youngest professional player in Korea by passing the Professional Qualification Tournament. But, in Japan, I was no match for them. It was the time of losing streak and I ended up in a blood match every time I played against any one of them.

When I was just starting out and lost the first game, and the second game, I was furious and I felt I did not deserve to lose. But the sense of defeat became more manageable as I lost many more games over and over again. I developed the mental strength to take blows well. And with every game, I played progressively better. Over time, I was not only catching up but playing at par with Kobayashi and Cho Chikun. I even started to win a game or two, which was a great feeling. As a 2P, I almost made it to the main tournament of the Meijin Championship and the Japanese Honinbo Title Match, which were the two most prestigious Go championships in Japan then. In the year I turned 17, Nihon Ki-in made me the rookie of the year. I was awarded with the Go-do award for holding 33 wins, one tie, and five losses.

I went from strength-to-strength when I returned to Korea. I conquered every championship, one by one, starting with the Choegowi Title Match. In 1980, I became the first in the history of international Go to win the grand slam. I was able to revive the glory of the grand slam in the years 1982 and 1986. I was also taking all the momentum I could to every international championship; the Ing Cup, the Fujistu Cup World Go Championship, the Tongyang Securities Cup, and the Chunlan Cup World Professional Weiqi Championship. In 2002, I became the oldest winner in the history of the Samsung Fire & Marine Insurance World Masters Baduk and at the inaugural kt Cup. From the 1980s to 2000s, I was on a winning streak for two decades and with it came the title of the 'Korean master of Go.' Those two decades were my time, until young Go players, including my student, Lee Changho began to take the titles away from me.

Though I have less physical and mental strengths today, I still do my best to win. Sometimes I am forced to bet on high odds in a tight game, earning the reputation of being cutthroat. But it also meant that I still had the same sharpness. At this age, my desire to expand territory is still very much alive and at work.

I do not believe that the world is full of competition and that only the fittest gets to survive. But it is the attitude that counts. Working hard to expand one's territory in whatever area of expertise one chooses. The meaning of territorial expansion is not limited to being successful or getting ahead of others. In a larger sense, it means to make the most out of one's potential, living one's dream and finding the purpose of one's life.

We should keep asking what we live for and how we want to live. We must give every option a try in the hope of living a better and happier life tomorrow. If tough competitions are in the way, get in the race. Don't give up too soon, or come up with excuses to avoid the fight. Everyone deserves to see the full potential unleased and there is still much territory waiting to be conquered.

CHANGHO'S HALF-POINT GAME

To be perfectly candid, I was not so convinced that Changho would go far and one day become a world champion when he came to study under me. Changho was good at playing Go but showed no sign of a genius. He was nondescript and inarticulate. Changho also had trouble remembering the moves he had made in the game he had just played. And yet for some reason, I had a feeling I should not give up on him. I followed my gut feeling and decided to take Changho in.

It did not take long for me to realize that there was a striking difference in our styles. I liked to play offense with speed and wit. Changho, on the other hand, was slow, stable, and serious. His style stems from his personality; earnest, calm, and gentle. For the six years that he lived in my house, never once did he make any noise or cause trouble. Changho spent everyday studying Go without any complaints.

One day, Changho and I were reviewing a game he had played before. Changho chose to play safe as usual when there was a strategically better and cleverer alternative. I asked why.

"The move is impactful but likely to be overturned, whereas my choice guarantees me to win 100 times out of 100 games by at least half a point," he said.

"Your choice is not bad, but don't you think the other option is easier and simpler?"

Changho did not say anything but his expression told me that he did not want to give up his slow-but-certain strategy. In a mentoring relationship, it was common for the mentor and the student to mold each other, but that was not the case for us. Changho and I were different all the way to the marrow; I am agile but he is slow. I like to play offense, he likes to play defense. I am a risk-taker but he chooses to play safe.

One day, such 'difference' between us came to pose a huge threat to me. In 1988, at the 28th Choegowi Title Match, Lee Changho sat opposite me after beating all the high-rank players, one by one. It was the first-ever match between a teacher and the student in the history of Go in Korea. I succeeded in defending the title from Changho, but I lost one game in that best-of-five match. I was defeated for the first time in an official competition by Changho. He won by merely half a point.

Half a point. Half a point is not even visible on the Go board. There are only whole numbers like one, two, and three points on the board, not a fraction like half a point. And yet someone can win by half a point because of the compensation rule. In Go, the black player has the first mover advantage. The white player is compensated with six and a half points for playing second. Those six and a half points are included when adding up the scores at the end of the game, allowing the player to win by half a point.

Some thought Changho was very lucky to win by a mere half a point. No one would have imagined that a 14-year-old was capable of including that half-a-point in his meticulous planning. But I knew Changho. He did not win by half a point by coincidence. I also knew that I was the problem.

Was I ready to play against someone like Changho, who believed he could win 100 times out of 100 games by only half a point? It did not take long for me to find out the answer.

In 1989, Changho and I met again at the Guksu Title Match. I won again by three to one. But I also lost one round to Changho, again, by half a point. In 1990, the two of us met again as the title defender and contender at the finals of the Choegowi Title Match. But this time, I lost to Changho. I got defeated by Changho for the first time in my life at this match. We played a tight game which ended with a 2-2 tie that continued into the last and final fifth round. But I lost by half a point again.

Since then we played against each other numerous times for championship titles and at every critical moment I lost by half a point. The curse of the half-a-point seemed to present itself over and over again. Changho holds 188 wins and 119 losses against me. He is ahead of me. I won by half a point 5 times against Changho, while he won by half a point 20 times. Changho knew that I could be vulnerable by half a point. It was my Achilles heel. Changho learned on his own how to outplay his teacher and he did it in his own way.

Changho had worked very hard to defeat me. He analyzed my game records in detail, my playing pattern to identify my weakness, and put together a winning strategy. There were few players who were able to beat me until Changho came along. Changho aimed for my weak spot by using his supercomputer-like calculation capacity and with his impenetrable maneuvers of stones. He did not miss the half a point that was missing in my calculation.

This was a clash of two different approaches to Go. There was, and is, more than one way to get closer to the core of this ancient game of Go. The one Changho took was far different from the one I chose to take. Changho's way was the first of its kind. No one has played like him before. Changho was able to see my weakness that everyone, including myself, missed because he was different.

Changho had his own weaknesses, too, which would become the target of AlphaGo-fighting Lee Sedol's ruthless attack in the years to come. Sedol was only 12 years old– the fifth player to debut at such a young age- when he became a professional Go player.

The history of the game of Go has carried on in such a way. I was defeated by Changho, whose approach to Go is different from mine. Changho is then defeated by Sedol, who plays in his own style. Anybody who takes down Sedol would be most likely to have a different playing style. A new generation of young power is right behind Sedol. It can only mean that the advent of another new style of Go is not too far away.

In order for a particular approach to be well received, it has to win. And a fresh successful approach is never created overnight. It is the manifestation of tirelessly analyzing the opponent, the ability to catch the rival's weak spot, and the fearless readiness to target that weak spot. The new approach is a creative one, something nobody has had the capacity to imagine before.

I see how new approaches are created and applied in the real world, too. Political power, for example, shifts to an emerging leader with a new political idea. In business, companies must embrace changes and innovation to meet the demand of the day in order to survive. For this reason, the qualifications a company looks for in its potential employees are redefined with time. In the past, companies valued integrity and loyalty. Not long ago, academic achievement and extra-curricular activities were thought to be important. Today, companies look for someone with a well-rounded character and creativity. But even these qualifications are bound to change again.

At home, the roles of parents are redefined depending on what is relevant in that era. Husband-and-wife or parents-children relationships are redefined as well. The new way of parenting or taking care of each other, for example, must be embraced by all family members for everyone to be happy. The more conservative father with patriarchal values must learn to be less authoritarian. The more old-school mother who expects complete obedience from her children must learn to accept them as an independent human being.

To be successful, one needs to know what kind of 'style' one has. Is it something that everyone already has, or is it a refreshingly creative one? The strongest competitive edge is having a style or an approach that sets oneself apart from everyone else. This is something not to be forgotten. At the same time, one needs to be abreast with the next rising approach to doing things. It is very likely that this new approach is already gaining prevalence. Those who have the capacity to catch up with it will be ready for the future, or even lead it.

THE WHEELCHAIR FIGHT

At the dawn of 1986, fans of Go could not get their eyes off of a bizarre scene. Cho Chikun 9P showed up in the finals of the Kisei Title Match in Japan, in a wheelchair.

It turned out that Chikun had a fender-bender with a motorcycle as he was driving off from his Chiba home drive way a few days ago. But Chickun was hit again by a speeding van which came out of nowhere as he was getting out of his car to deal with the motorcycle. The van sped away, leaving Chickun seriously injured. He had a broken right shinbone that ripped through his flesh, torn left ligament patellae, fractured left wrist, and a wound on his head. Fortunately, CT results showed no damage was done to his brain.

The news of Chikun's accident threw the Japanese Go community into utter chaos. There was only a week left before the finals of the Kisei Title Match where Chikun was supposed to defend his title. When Chikun came out of the 15-hour surgery, he was bed-tied in a full-body cast. The host of the match was in great panic, considering whether to delay the game. But Chikun told them that he wanted to play as scheduled.

"I have no injury on my head and my right hand. This is a God-given sign saying that I should play. I am capable of playing right now."

Chikun was in his patient gown, wearing casts on his left leg and foot with a blanket covering his lap, when he appeared for the final match. It was obvious that he felt uncomfortable but he was adamant about playing.

The first round ended with his loss. He was probably stretching backwards to fight in such a condition in the first place. But Chikun dispelled all concerns. He impressed the spectators by winning the second and third rounds in a row. The second round he played on that day, in particular, is still much talked about. It was recorded as one of the best in the history of Go. All observers were in disbelief. Chikun did not just manage the game. It was executed beautifully.

In the end, Chikun lost by 2-4. The Kisei Title Match was the last of the Big Three titles Chikun had to defend after losing the Japanese Honinbo Title Match and the Meijin Championship. By losing the Kisei Title, the emperor of Go was left crownless. Nevertheless, no one laughed at him. Everybody was deeply inspired by the astonishing fighting spirit that he had exerted. And there was one more hero at the scene. It was Kobayashi, the contender and the man who put me through hell in the quarterfinals of the first Ing Cup.

In the history of Japanese Go, Chikun and Kobayashi were considered to be old foes. The two studied Go at the Minoru Kitani's Go school around the same time and spent their childhood together at the Fujisawa study group. It was at the Fujisawa study group that I met with Chikun and Kobayashi.

Of the two, the first one to stand out was Chikun. At the age of 24, he defeated Hideo Otake and won the Meijin Championship. From there, he took it all the way to the top, taking over one by one the Big Three titles in Japanese Go. Kobayashi was the man Chikun had always feared the most. And he waited for Kobayashi at the top. Chikun mentioned once in an interview that he revered those who never stopped endeavoring every day to reach the top. Chikun, I believe, was referring to Kobayashi.

In 1985, the two rivals finally met. Kobayashi defeated all of the star players and sat before Chikun at the Meijin Championship. Kobayashi, who had been waiting for that moment, quickly went after Chikun as soon as the timer started to tick. Chikun managed to shake off the pursuit with difficulty and persevered into the 7th round but did not make it in the final round. Kobayashi started to go all-out to take down Chikun. Chikun lost the titles he held, one by one, whereas Kobayashi won the Triple Crown-the Judan Title match, the Meijin Championship, and the Tengen Title Match. In 1986, Kobayashi fought Chikun for the Kisei Title, which was Chikun's last remaining title.

How Kobayashi must have felt when the archrival of his life showed up in the long-awaited match with a full-body cast in a wheelchair, I could not imagine. The average person would have been unwilling to fight against a wounded opponent. Win or lose, playing against a wounded man did not seem to be worth the trouble either way; the assumption being an easy win, or a carless loss. But Kobayashi was not an average man. When he paid a visit to see Chikun in the hospital, Kobayashi accepted his decision to fight as scheduled. On the day of the match, Kobayashi gave his best without pulling a punch.

Both Chikun and Kobayashi later mentioned about the Kisei Title Match in their memoirs as well as in several interviews. Kobayashi said "Chikun was stronger than ever in a wheelchair. He was asking to fight on an equal footing." To Kobayashi, Chikun was not a wounded man, but a powerful rival as he has always been. There was no reason for Kobayashi to spare his best out of pity for Chikun. Chikun put up a strong fight and so did Kobayashi.

"I believe it was Kobayashi who was put in an unfavorable position, not me. It must have been awkward to fight against an injured opponent. But Kobayashi did not go easy on me. He fought hard to win. There were only a few people who could do the same," said Chikun. He added, "I was strong. Tough enough to win the game but I lost. That was my limit. I have never blamed the accident for my defeat."

It is not the powerful who wins, but whoever wins becomes the powerful one. I applaud both Chikun and Kobayashi; Chikun, for not giving up even when he was wheelchair-bound, and Kobayashi, for his professionalism. At one glance, Kobayashi seemed to have the upper hand but it was not true at all. It was a fair and close game, where only one could be the winner. That was all there was to it.

A truly strong person never makes an excuse. Someone who has worked very hard to win can accept defeat gracefully. If one loses, that is because the opponent is stronger. Accept the fact, move on and work harder. I believe that the most important professional courtesy a master of Go must demonstrate is to do one's best in a match. Expressing to resign long before the end of the game or playing halfheartedly because the opponent appears to be less experienced are not the attitude expected of a professional player. Never look down on the opponent. No one appreciates an easy win against an opponent who is half-serious about the game. What is appreciated is professionalism, accepting the opponent as equally competitive and doing one's best to win.

For this reason, I give my best at every game. Although I have come to make more mistakes with age, I have never been unenthusiastic about games. I believe being enthusiastic and serious are simply professional courtesy.

In the 2001 Samsung Fire & Marine Insurance World Masters Baduk, I defeated Chang Hao, China's top Go player, and won the championship. Chinese reporters complained that I, an old man, was standing in the way of young Chinese players. "Haven't you enjoyed enough wealth and fame? Don't you think it is time for you to stand aside and let young Chinese player win?" one of the reporters asked.

After a moment of thought, I replied. "I believe I am doing a favor to the Chinese Go and the Chinese players by doing my best at every game." The Chinese reporters did not reply back. Perhaps they had an epiphany about the meaning of true sportsmanship.

TORNADOS RIDE ON
THE ASCENDING CURRENT

A fierce but invisible battle of two colliding energies takes place on the Go board. Sometimes I feel that my opponent does not confront my provocation but chooses to turn tail because he does not know what to do. Not every challenge has to be accepted, of course. There is, however, a clear distinction between ignoring a provocation and running away. The former is the outcome of confidence, high spirit, and has a triumphant note, whereas the latter is a sign of nervousness, anxiety, and even servility. When these two opposing dynamics are felt in the air, it seems the winner and the loser is pre-determined before the game is even over. No matter how skilled a player is, no one can play at one's best when psychologically intimidated.

To win, a player has to have first and foremost a fighting spirit. One must be full of confidence and show it in every way. One should not be intimidated no matter how great an opponent one meets. As soon as one shows fear, the opponent will jump at the opportunity to display more strength.

Energy is mysterious in nature. It is invisible and intangible but definitely felt. Whether one is full of confidence or feeling a shadow of anxiety is noticeable. What is more inexplicable is that the more frightened, the weaker one becomes, while the more confident, the stronger one becomes. The mechanism works like a tornado that gets more powerful with more ascending air current.

Energy between two individuals affects each other. An anxious individual feels more insecure in the presence of an audacious individual. On the contrary, a self-confident individual becomes more self-assured by preying on the anxiety of others. In a nutshell, the more one feels anxious the stronger the opponent becomes. Nothing expedites a KO than stepping into the boxing ring already frightened. One must believe in oneself and have the guts to confront the opponent with the 'Let's fight. Bring it on!' mentality.

In this respect, winning the Ing Cup may be attributable to the fighting spirit I had shown at the competition. But, in fact, I was not brimming with confidence from the beginning because I did not think I stood a chance to win with any of the players. But I kept talking to myself that there was always a chance to win if I played at my best without making any mistakes. All I needed to do was to play my own game and be in control of it, and I expected my opponent would do the same.

I learned how powerful self-confidence could be while going through the quarterfinals of the Ing Cup, playing against with Kobayashi who had inflicted a humiliating defeat on me in the first round of the Fujistu Cup World Go Championship a few months earlier. The defeat in the Fujitsu Cup was even more painful because all three Korean Go players including myself lost in the first round. Even the media prematurely concluded that Korea still had a long way to go.

But the experience of that bitter first round gave me just enough confidence to think that the next game would be worth a try. Sure, the Japanese and the Korean Go players played at different levels, but the gap was not something insurmountable. We could have stayed longer in the tournament if it weren't for the few careless mistakes and miscalculation of the moves. We could have even won some rounds. Perhaps what we really needed was experience and confidence. So I decided to have faith in my Go skill when I met Kobayashi in the quarterfinal of the Ing Cup. I thought I had a chance to beat even a high-profile player like Kobayashi if I could just relax and stay focused.

Kobayashi was an extremely tough opponent. Even now, my brain is on the verge of imploding thinking of that game I played against him. But I realized that trusting myself helped me to bear the countless tense moments in that game. Half-way through, I made a single mistake that almost jeopardized the entire game but I hung on until the perfect moment to strike back came. And when it did, I launched a series of bold attacks towards the end of the game because I knew I had nothing to lose. Perhaps Kobayashi was startled by my guts? Kobayashi seemed apprehensive and started to retreat…and I felt it.

When the board was covered with the stones and the counting of the scores was finally over, everyone could not believe their eyes. Everybody assumed that I was losing. But when the scores were counted using the Ing Cup rule, the result said otherwise. I won and I moved on to the semifinal. The victory tasted sweeter than ever because Kobayashi was not easy. And I felt more confident about myself.

Riding on the momentum, I faced Rin Kaiho, a.k.a. 'double waists', in the semifinal. Rin Kaiho earned his nickname from his tenacious style. Rin Kaiho was famous for building thick stone groups that could not be halved with a single swing of a sword. His move is seemingly slow and dull, but actually well-informed and exhaustive, leaving little chance to make a mistake. Knowing that prolonged game would reduce my chance to win, I tried to lead the game with speed and a nonstop blitz.

Who said that his Go was dull? Rin Kaiho was a cold-hearted master swordsman. One deep stab was painful enough to lose consciousness. What appeared like a peaceful game was in fact a bloody battle of fatal attacks and desperate defenses. I tried to stay focused and to be in control of myself. I bombarded him with as many attacks I could come up with. Final tally confirmed my victory by five points.

I continued on to the finals. I won the first round but lost the next two rounds to Nie Weiping. I knew that nothing was conclusive at that point. I still had two more rounds to go and I believed there was a fair chance to win if I was able to be myself no matter how he played. I think Nie Weiping felt my determination. He must have wondered how a no-name Go player from nowhere like me could be so dauntless in the presence of the emperor of Go like himself, who has a track record of crushing so many big names. Confused and distressed, Nie Weiping could have felt too much pressure that he decided to throw his stone and resign. It all came down to who was more valiant and unshaken, rather than who played better, that ultimately determined the winner. The trophy of the champion went to the one who did not break under pressure.

In sports, in general, spectators are able to tell which team has the drive to win. The moment the spectators catch that energy, the game quickly turns around in that team's favor. Such turnaround is commonly referred to as the 'flow of the game', but I like to call it 'riding on the ascending current.' The impact of displaying high spirit is so powerful that athletes do so on purpose during a game to intimidate the other side. In combat sports, fighters throw their fists in the air and grunt as loud as they can, or tennis players exert a guttural grunt with each serve. Grunting in sports can have the effect of overwhelming the opponent. The more conspicuous the display of confidence is, the stronger the whirlwind grows, which can be a build-up to victory.

In the everyday life, every move must be made with confidence; all the more so, if one is at a critical juncture. Confident facial expression or posture can bring positive energy. Anyone who has experienced it will understand what I am talking about. It is truly amazing. Self-confidence partly stems from hypnotizing oneself to feel confident. It is also a healthy narcissism. Keep repeating the magic mantra every day; "I can do it. I am no less than others." If it helps, get dressed in the best outfit and groom yourself. I find myself walking in lighter steps, with my shoulders back, and head high in a white dress shirt and colorful necktie that my children gave me as gifts. So in a funny way, confidence can be purchased at the mall.

Above all, create as many opportunities to build confidence as possible; take tests, go out and network, do presentations in front of a large audience. Take on more challenging and unfamiliar tasks. These help to work in smarter and skillful ways. Making silly mistakes or being criticized for things that go wrong can be discouraging but are part of the journey. Each experience is a build-up to opportunities to become successful and more confident. Losing is a prerequisite to win. Only those who are not afraid of being defeated will have the opportunity to win.

Never be intimidated by anyone under any circumstances. Keep shoulders back and let out a loud grunt. Victory is already in your hands.

"The game is over the moment
those two stones are placed on the board.
But resignation means lost opportunities… and lost possibilities.
So one must not end the game, just not yet."

Chapter 4

Go
with
the Flow

RIGHT HERE, RIGHT NOW

I encountered a language barrier in my own country, Korea, when I returned from Japan. 9 years in Japan was more than enough to almost completely forget my mother tongue. I managed to remember a few words like 'mom' and 'dad' but forgot the words for 'older sister' and 'younger brother' in Korean. It took me a while even to recall simple words like 'water.' I had no problem communicating with my parents because they spoke Japanese, but I had problem getting by outside the house.

Those at the Go club– older than me or around the same age looked at me with curious eyes as I could not understand even simple words. Some of them were mischievous enough to approach me under the pretense of helping me learn Korean, but instead taught me inappropriate words on purpose to get me into trouble. People burst out laughing at my mistakes and my feelings were hurt. I gradually became tight-lipped and often had a long face. I had always been an outgoing and social person, but found myself retreating ever since I came back to Korea. I always wore a big smile in the photos taken while studying in Japan unlike the ones taken in

Korea. I rarely smiled in those.

Language barrier was not the only problem I encountered. The Go clubs in Korea were very different from the ones in Japan. In Japan, it was natural to sit down with peers to review moves and talk about strategies at the Go club, whereas in Korea, Go clubs seemed to exist for nothing else but the sole purpose of playing games. At the Korean Go club, I had to 'sit-and-play' right away with the first person I made eye contact with and lunch would be on the person who loses. I went to the Go club every day and regularly participated in competitions, but I had a hard time settling down. My game records came out to be not so impressive. I was waiting to be drafted to the Army to do my mandatory service as a Korean citizen and at the same time feeling uprooted and replanted in a completely different world. I was still between Japan and Korea.

Everyone in Japan strictly observed good manners when playing Go. It was no exception even when we played quick games. No one looked down at me or treated me like a child during games in Japan because I was young. Rather, I was treated with respect for studying under the 'great' Kensaku Segoe. Politicians, high-ranking officers, and businessmen who visited Master Segoe's house kneeled down and bowed at me according to the etiquettes of Japanese Go, saying "Sensei Cho, please allow me to join you for a game of Go," when they wished to play with me.

I was humbled to be respected in such a way by gentlemen who were my senior in age. They took the culture of courtesy built around Go seriously and I believed in it. I reciprocated as I was taught in that culture, by accepting their request with modesty and mutual respect. Their politeness was not supposed to make me feel elated or ignite a sense of arrogance in me. The virtual circle of courtesy in the game of Go is nurtured in such a way.

I was confused when I shifted to a different culture in Korea. Wherever I went, people asked how old I was. They were very quick to treat me like a child when they learned I was only nineteen. I had to be conscious of other people's age, too, to properly address them according to seniority. I had to learn the delicate difference between appellations for formal and informal hierarchal interpersonal relationships. For example, how to address someone my senior as a 'big brother,' 'sunbae, ' 'Mister.' Sometimes, I had to deal with the rich and well-connected people who swung by the Go club and called me out loud, as if they were hailing a cab. "Hey, Cho! Come here and play a game with me."

Kim In sunbae, who was my senior at the Go club, came to my rescue. Kim In sunbae was the man who opened a new era in the history of Korean Go. He loved to drink and was a skilled calligrapher. Kim In sunbae considered the game of Go to be a form of art. And he had the soul of an artist. Kim In sunbae was obsessed with the quality of the games he played. He never hesitated to resign if he was not on top of his game, even if he had the upper hand. I never mentioned a word to Kim In sunbae but he knew exactly what I was going through. Kim In sunbae himself had studied for 2 years at the legendary Minoru Kitani School before I did and we came from the same region in Korea. Having a common background, perhaps he felt a sense of brotherhood. He took me out for a drink, or to climb the mountain, to help me put things into perspective.

"It is true that the Japanese Go puts more emphasis on the pursuit of self-enlightenment and practicing courtesy while the Korean Go looks more or less like a battlefield. Neither is wrong, nor better than the other. They are just different. When in Japan, you accepted the Japanese practices. Likewise, embrace the Korean approach when in Korea."

Kim In sunbae added that the disorderly battlefield style may be the fast track for Korean Go to become competitive.

He was right. A decade later, Korean Go had advanced to top ranks in the world whereas the Japanese Go had been on a downhill. Korea's battlefield approach had succeeded in establishing a great system of promoting healthy competition among players while Japan remained obsessed with formalities. Kim In sunbae was convincing and I stopped pushing away people who wanted to play Go with me.

In retrospect, he was right about the cultural differences between the Korean and Japanese Go. It was natural to ask one's age in Korea because of the social and cultural practice of respecting those who are one's senior even if there is only a few months difference in age. Having once studied under Master Segoe did not mean anything in the social hierarchy in Korea. I was a 19-year-old young adult. Over time, I became fond of betting lunch over Go games and used it to work on skills that I can actually apply at competitions.

Master Shuko Fujisawa, who deeply cared about me, was very sad when I left Japan. He described my departure as abandoning the fertile soil for a barren land. He lamented that I, a diamond in the rough, was never going to get a chance to be cut, polished and discovered in Korea. I believe, however, that the wilderness full of savage dogs turned out to be the best training environment for me. Master Fujisawa was happier than anyone else when I won the Ing Cup and ever since then, he became a big fan of Korean Go.

We are inclined to look for alternatives when we are dissatisfied with where we are today. I have learned, however, the importance of where we are right now. Blaming our unhappiness on the environment will change nothing. If we are dissatisfied, we have the choice of working hard to make changes and make a difference.

The only thing that should be on the mind when playing Go is where to play. One must concentrate all the mental strength to figure out the positions on the game board. In real life, likewise, one must appreciate the present. Be in the moment because it will never come back again. Every dream begins 'right here, right now.'

OUTSIDE IN

There is a saying among Go players that one has the advantage by eight points from looking at the game outside in. A spectator is able to see eight moves ahead and have a bird's eye view of the game than the players themselves. It is often the case that the players are obsessed with winning the game, so much so that they are unable to have an accurate reading of the game and miss the opportunity to win. Believing to be at a disadvantage, one may choose to avoid placing the stones on certain positions to play safe during the game, not realizing that one is actually ahead of the opponent. The lesson here is that being too immersed in the game one misses the chance to make the move that could have led to defeating the opponent. "How did I miss it?" The realization may arrive too late.

In real life, as one minds one's own business, one is inclined to exaggerate one's problems and unhappiness. One wonders why everyone else has an affluent upbringing, is good looking, articulate, and social? Everyone around seems to be able to afford a house and a car at such a young age when one is still struggling to make a breakthrough.

But others maybe feeling the same way. They may be noticing one's likeable character, well-paid job, and girlfriend who has all the desirable qualities with a hint of jealousy. One's life appears to be going well from a distance.

That is life. Life seems to be unfair at first glance, but in relative terms, it is fair. Everyone wants more and is envious of the achievements of others. But how many people are actually capable of turning jealousy and envy into setting goals and achieving them? Most people do not go any further than complaining. But the brave ones jump over that wall to climb to the top. They choose to become someone who is no longer envious of others.

Cha Minsu, also known as Jimmy Cha, was a professional Go player and a gambler. His life story was so interesting and unique that it was made into a television drama in Korea. I met Minsu at a Go club when I returned from Japan. I was shy, had a hard time talking to strangers, and not so conversant in Korean. On the other hand, Minsu was a charming, confident, and approachable young man with a great smile, who was able to have a conversation with anyone. When I met Minsu for the first time, he had not yet taken the Professional Qualification Tournament, nevertheless, he was already widely known as the armature player who posed a threat to professional players.

Minsu and I became close friends while we served in the Air Force together. I was expecting to be drafted for military service soon after I returned to Korea but I had to wait for the conscription office to start the process. When I grew tired of waiting, I volunteered to join the Air Force. My first post was the Seongnam airfield and I was later transferred to the Office of Education and Training at the Air University in Daebang-dong, Seoul. It was at the PX of the university that I ran into Minsu.

Minsu had already made a name for himself. In only a few months after passing the qualification test to play professional Go, he had already defeated every single officer at the university. I received a special order to beat Minsu as a payback. I was supposed to be the secret weapon, but I ended up losing to him by one point. Minsu was good, but what was truly amazing was his powerful energy and high spirit. He was 1P and I, 6P, but he did not feel intimidated at all by my rank. Ever since then, Minsu and I

Life works in unpredictable ways. One can start out with nothing,
but ends up with everything the next day.
If one succumbs to grief and despair, the game ends there.
But the game continues as long as one has the will to stay in it.

played a quick game whenever we met to catch up with each other. Over the course of my military service, I ended up playing about a hundred or more quick games with Minsu. They served as good practice games to prepare me for Go competitions that I participated in during the period of my service.

I expected Minsu to be a Go sensation as soon as he was discharged from the military, sweeping up the trophies in competitions. He seemed to have the perfect package; he was good looking, came from an affluent family, and was talented in many things. He swam, played table tennis, played the piano and the violin, in addition to playing Go. He had a brilliant mind that was capable of absorbing anything he learned like a dry sponge and easily conquered it. He had everything going for him and the Go board was too small for his passion. To my surprise, Minsu decided to emigrate to the U.S. when he was discharged. He started a new career as a professional gambler in the U.S.

Years of blood, sweat and tears paid off. Minsu became very successful in professional gambling, earning a whopping annual income of approximately 4 million dollars in his heydays. But Minsu had to go through twists and turns before he became successful. When Minsu was going from strength to strength as a professional gambler, I paid a visit to see him in the U.S. As for me, I had then lost the last championship title I had to Changho.

Minsu was living a happy life with his wife and children in a magnificent mansion. He was still the confident man that I had always known.

One evening, as we were catching up with each other, I saw his eyes turn red. Minsu told me about the story of his first marriage that failed. Minsu lost everything he had to his ex-wife, including the custody of his children, when he got divorced. He came back to Korea destitute that he had to live moving from one shabby inn to another for nearly half a year.

"I had no idea that a human body contained so much moistures. I cried all day but tears never seem to dry up."

When Minsu returned to the U.S., he had nothing but 18 dollars in his pocket. He played Go for 20 dollars per round until he scraped together 1,600 dollars. Minsu took this money and ran to a casino where his real games began. He buckled down with clenched teeth and gambled to stay alive. Minsu wanted to get his life back and little by little, he regained hope. Along the way, he met his second wife and settled down to start a family.

Minsu is a versatile man; he now coaches the national Go team in Korea while still playing professional Go, in addition to managing his casino business. People are envious of his huge success. But they often forget how life used to be an ordeal for him before his breakthrough came. When asked how he endured his darkest moments, he said, "After much contemplation, I realized that it was not the worst. True, I lost everything, but at least I was healthy. I knew how to gamble for a living, and I had people who had faith in me. I convinced myself that I had enough resources to be on my feet again. If I were too caught up with the fact that I had failed, I would have rather died. But I realized that I still had a shot when I took a step back and looked at my situation. I pulled myself together and started to work intensely."

I was able to relate to Minsu right away because I was in the same place as him. I had lost every single title I had, but I had not lost any of my fingers nor was my brain seriously injured. The fact that there was nothing to keep helped to take things easy.

Life works in unpredictable ways. One can start out with nothing, but ends up with everything the next day. If one succumbs to grief and despair, the game ends there. But the game continues as long as one has the will to stay in it.

The world beneath our feet is a huge Go board. The moment we place those two stones on the board, the game is over. What a shame, when we have not yet used up all of our chances. One may be in distressed, believing that one has exhausted every means to get back in the game. But those onlookers watching over our shoulders think otherwise. There are enough stones to make one's moves. So the game must go on.

DREAMS COME AT A COST

One day, as I was getting ready to head to the Go club, I asked my mother for some money for transportation. I noticed a sense of embarrassment flashed across her face. "Wait a moment," she said.

I saw my mom run next door to borrow some money. I used to take a cab then because I didn't know my way around Seoul. I had a strange feeling while riding the taxi to the Go club that soon translated into a sense of responsibility. It dawned on me that it was about time that I started to make money for a living.

I had never really thought about earning money up to that time. My family was poor but I never had to worry about money. I knew that my parents tried to make ends meet selling vegetables in the market, but I was not worried about being poor. Being poor was not something to be concerned about because everyone was poor in Korea back then. Besides, I was able to study in Japan and finish my training with little difficulty because individuals and organizations who appreciated my talent sponsored me. Chosun Daily Newspaper paid for the round trip airfare and many Koreans living in Japan took care of me.

But, to me, Master Segoe was the most generous sponsor and supporter. In theory, studying under someone's tutelage was supposed to be free but in practice, students were sometimes asked to pay for food and accommodation. Those who could not afford to pay in advance, or who were not obliged to pay for anything, would come back years later after they have become successful to pay back in a symbolic amount. But Master Segoe never asked a single penny from me nor my parents during the 9 years I lived with him.

"You will study under me starting today," was all he said to allow me to become his student. Instead of asking me for compensation, Master Segoe asked Mama zzang, his daughter-in-law, to give me a few thousand yen of allowance every month.

My life in Japan was better off than in Korea; I lived in a better house with plenty of food to eat and was never short of anything. Most of all, I did not feel the pinch because there was no need to pay anything myself. I had been spoiled with a comfortable life in Japan that even at 20, I did not comprehend what being poor or earning for a living meant. I was briefly surprised by the humble house my family lived in and their shabby cloths when I returned to Korea, but I assumed it was because of the difference in the living standards between the two countries. I was not able to make the connection between what I saw and the financial situation my family was in. I snapped out of a superficial life upon seeing my mother borrow money for something so trifling as transportation.

'We are really poor. I should earn money to help out my family,' I thought.

It is often said that a boy becomes a man only when he starts to worry about making money for a living. I had a moment of epiphany. I realized that playing Go was my job and that I had to make money from it.

A few months later, just before I joined the Air Force, I won the Choegowi Title Match sponsored by the Busan Daily Newspaper. Not only did I win, but I also earned prize money for the first time in my life. 300,000 won in prize money was worth a significant amount back then. I gave the money to my mother. The timing could not have been more right. My sister had just been accepted to an art program at a university which meant my mother could really use some money to pay for my sister's college and art supplies.

Since that day, I never forgot that I was playing Go to put food on the table. It was more so because my parents and siblings had made sacrifices for me. The sense of responsibility grew stronger when I got married and the children were born. The more championship titles I won, the more things we were able to afford. I was able to pay for my children's school which kept rising with grade. We also moved to a better and larger house. There were times when I was too exhausted and felt like squatting down to let things take its own course. But I could not allow myself to do so because I had a family to support. I believe anyone who has children would understand the weight of life weighing on my shoulders. Sometimes money is a powerful motivation.

How would one feel if the reward at the end of a strenuous climbing is trifling? In the world of professional Go, reward is all the more important. Prize money, in particular, is the real tangible reward for all the hard work. Why is annual salary negotiation a sensitive issue in professional sports? The reason is because value is placed on the achievement- or the perceived achievement- of the athlete. Higher salary and favorable terms and conditions are direct reflections of how much the athlete is worth. If hard work is not paid off with actual reward, who would be interested in working hard to make their dreams come true? When the rewards are clearly defined, the motivation becomes stronger to set specific goals and work towards accomplishing it. 'I shall work hard to rise and shine and make my family happy.'

The game of Go was everything to me; it was the very means of making a living, my dream, and my path to self-fulfillment. I appreciated and enjoyed the rewards of breaking my back. I realized that a dream and a job are not necessarily the same for many people. In this respect, I felt very lucky that I loved what I did for a living. For those whose jobs are not necessarily their passion, there is still room to have a dream. Our parents did their best every single day because they replaced their original dreams with new one that was to provide a brighter future for their children so that they have much more chance to realize what their parents dreamed about. Hard work can be rewarded in this way.

Having a dream that is different from one's job, therefore, is not something to agonize over. It is not too late to start dreaming now doing what one does for a living. In fact, there is nothing more important than paying the bills because basic needs have to be met for anyone to afford a dream. In this sense, having a job could be a dream, too. It may not sound like an exciting dream, relatively speaking, but that is not the reason to feel small about it. So, take it from there. Anyone is entitled to have a dream, to endeavor to make it come true, and rightfully expect the rewards of devotion. Hard work will accrue until one day, one finds doing what one has always dreamed of doing.

TAKE IT FROM THE MASTER

There is a famous story retold among Go players. Ten 9 Kyu players are sitting around the Go board deep in thought. Where can the stones be placed to avoid trouble? They have been thinking over carefully for about an hour but to no avail. Suddenly, a 1 Kyu player comes along, takes a look at the board for a brief 10 seconds and says, "Hey, put this stone over here and you are safe."

The difference between each Kyu is significant. Someone who plays at a higher level is capable of finding the empty spot right away. The same goes for someone who is a professional and someone who is an amateur. What is the difference between amateurs and professionals? Simply put, the levels of their knowledge, theories, and skills are the key differences. But the fundamental difference lies in their ability to 'read the game, or the situation.' The ability to read the game improves in precision progressively with each level of Go.

The ability to read the situation accurately becomes much more critical in the battlefield. A 16th century Korean naval commander who lived in the age of Joseon Dynasty, Admiral Yi Sunshin, was never defeated while fighting as many as 45 battles during the Imjin War, the 1592-1598 Japanese Invasion of Korea. Despite being outnumbered in ships, 13 to 130, Yi Sunshin destroyed Japanese warships without losing a single one of his own at the Battle of Myeongnyang. His victory was attributable to his near-perfect strategy which was based on his deep insight into everything relevant in the battle, including the geographic features, the weather conditions, and the enemy's tactics.

Hence, the leader in charge is called the 'general.' The word 'general' is widely used to mean 'ordinary' or 'common,' but it also means to 'have a comprehensive knowledge and perspective.' In other words, the general of an armed forces is called a 'general' because that individual has the outstanding ability to read the situation and anticipate how events would unfold at the battlefield.

Such 'general' approach is much needed in every corner of our society. A politician should keep a balance between economic growth and wealth distribution between the haves and the have-nots. A diplomat should not be preoccupied by a side issue with a single country. A strategically meaningful, informed decision must be made after factoring in all relevant aspects that affect diplomatic relationships, such as international political situation, and the dynamics between stakeholders and neighbors. Entrepreneurs must be abreast with the political, social, economic, and cultural trends in the world and quickly adapt to those changes to not only survive but to stay ahead of others.

Beginners fall short in this particular ability to do a comprehensive reading of the situation. They are engrossed in a frivolous Ko fight or a stone group fight that they often fail to see the big picture. Anybody who plays Go knows very well the board is larger than it appears. It can accommodate limitless combinations of variables and territories. When fierce attacks are made in one corner, there is a desperate attempt to resist in another, while in another corner, the decision must be made either to retrieve now to reclaim the point later, or to hold one's position until the end. Each area looks independent and disconnected but they will eventually become connected influencing each other. Being a master means understanding the intricate invisible links between the territories and being able to build new links. Every stone on the board serves a purpose, which is why they need to be organically connected to each other and accounted for in the decision-making process.

The ability to coordinate the moves of each stone could be 'leadership.' A master must be in control of the stones on the board while a beginner is likely to move the stones around in confusion until things become totally out of control. The primary reason is because a beginner has not yet developed a strong sense of judgement and leadership to manage a crisis in the overall context of what is happening on the board. Beginners who are aware of this shortcoming push themselves to analyze game records, know theories by heart, and play as many games as possible to qualify for higher level. Furthermore, they understand very well that the fast track to hone their skills is to play against someone at a higher level and learn from losing. As such, in the world of Go, regardless of age and gender, anyone above one's level deserves to be respected.

What about in the real world? Do beginners listen to the experienced and show respect to them? I have seen many who have lost their respect for the expert; students who are disrespectful to their teachers, children who never listen to their parents, employees who talk behind their employers, and juniors who think they know better than their seniors.

The mindset and the behavior of the older generation may appear outdated to the eyes of the young. Prioritizing formalities over substance, process over the end result, or adamant adherence to the old way of doing things may cause frustration. Repeated disappointment eats away the initial respect and gradually turns into disregard. Unfortunately, the eagerness and the willingness to learn everything and anything diminish at the same time. New recruits are all ears to their managers, writing down every single word spoken they hear. 2 to 3 years into their job, they become overconfident and start dismissing the advice of their managers as annoying interference.

When new young managers take over the positions years later, they finally realize what their predecessors have been trying to say. One is capable of understanding only what one can see. One also makes the mistake of believing that one sees everything, hence, knows it all. Such conviction is the culprit of diminished modesty and failure to remember one's humble beginning.

A piece of advice from someone with more experience, however, is worth listening. Their advice has been attested by repeated experiences. A junior, in an organization, is simply assigned to do a job. But a teacher or a manager are the ones with the bird's eye view of the organization, capable of seeing further and wider. They see everyone in the organization and have a clear idea of what is happening. They see the situation as a whole, and can put events in context. They can be trusted; there is always a good reason when they choose to do things in a certain way. As an old Korean saying puts it, advice given by one's senior is never wrong. An arrogant individual could never become a master. Only those who are eager to learn will become masters.

A master is someone who has already walked the numerous paths a beginner has not yet seen. A beginner panics when trying to put out the fire on his feet whereas a master could do so in a calm way and still be able to make other plans and decisions. Anyone who wants to become a master must acknowledge this difference and strive to learn from the master with the consistent willingness to acquire more. That day will eventually come when one is called the master.

GIVE IT UP

The 'Ten Commandments' in Go was compiled by Wang Jeoksin, a Kidaejo, or a servant designated to play Go with the emperor, to Emperor Xuanzong of Qing Dynasty, China. The 5th commandment says, 'one shall not trade a dollar for a penny,' meaning one shall enjoy bigger benefit by giving up small gain. There is also a four-character idiom related to Go that has the same message; 'penny-wise and pound-foolish,' which means 'to incur a great loss by pursuing a small profit'.

If a respected individual advises people not to trade a dollar for a penny, everyone would say, "Of course, I will listen to you." However, easier said than done. Giving up can be harder than expected when a small benefit comes into sight within a reachable distance. It is a shame that one may even lose the opportunity to gain larger profit by being caught up on a small one. How 'penny-wise and pound-foolish!'

One must read the game as accurately as possible to avoid making such mistakes. Beginners often indulge in the fun of catching the opponent's stones that they let the opponent to capture their large stone groups and conquer their territories. Such disposition maybe used by experienced players. Master players may let the beginners catch a few of their stones as a bait, the most common one being distracting them with the pleasure of Ponnuki, capturing the opponent's stones with four stones. They will then quietly expand their territories while the beginners are still lost in Ponnuki.

The Ten Commandments primarily talks about the 6th commandment, 'when in danger, abandon the stone' tells one to give up the stones when at risk, and the 10th, 'seek harmony when isolated" tells one to pursue a peaceful engagement rather than resisting and risking annihilation. The Ten Commandments sound like riddles and are too abstract even for me to have a thorough understanding of them, but time and again I find them to be very relevant in real life, too. The Ten Commandments taught me the wisdom of life, to let go trivial matters. There are times when surrendering or relinquishing bring unintended advantages and benefits in the future.

People have come to me making offers in unexpected ways; business proposals, appearance in commercial advertisement, and even a high-ranking position in an organization. All of them sounded great and promised significant benefits. But it did not feel right to willingly accept them because of the possible consequences they could have on my professional career and my reputation. I rejected most of them out of concern for their impact on my life-long achievement.

There were times, however, when I regretted not accepting the invitations to make a fortune or fame. They were very tempting and I am only human with many flaws. But I always looked back and told myself that I had done the right thing. No economic benefit could replace my love for Go. My gut feeling tells me that if I had those offers, I could have become disconnected from Go.

The game of Go is played between the Black and the White, each with about 180 stones, confined to a space specifically made for the game, with a time limit. Players are conditioned to place their stones in the most effective and efficient ways within the restrictions while looking at the big picture and estimating the end result. As such, the ability to prioritize is critical. One has to be wise to give up what is not within reach and brave to sacrifice one stone for a bigger return.

This is more than mere a game tip. It can be applied to real life. A choice has an impact on what follows. Every temptation, no matter how small, comes with a price. Resist giving into a small temptation for a bigger opportunity to be successful. Take a step back and get a larger view to see what the priority in one's life is. The hint is in every single corner of the board.

Release oneself from the things that tie one down. Shrug it off. Lighten the body and the mind to travel faster, longer, and further.

"Go players are trained to never make a bad move,

which is almost impossible in real life.

Sometimes one is forced to place a stone on the wrong place knowing very well

that it was going to be the wrong move."

Chapter 5

Look Far Ahead into the Future

THE PRICE OF SPEED

The standard time limit in Go used to be long hours in the past. Nowadays, the time limit is reduced to 2 to 3 hours, not exceeding 4 to 7 hours at most. Two decades ago, the time limit for each player was 5 hours. Combined with hours of overtime counting, total number of hours easily surpassed 11 hours. I still vividly remember the 1993 final game in the Kisung Title Match that I played against my student, Changho. We played 7 rounds and every one of them ended after 11 o'clock at night. Those were probably the longest Go games ever played in the history of Korea.

Even today, the Japanese are famous for playing long hours. The time limit for all three major title matches, the Kisei, the Meijin, and the Japanese Honinbo, is eight hours per player, which adds up to 16 hours of game time all together. To accommodate the time limit, it was decided to extend the duration of one round to two days. For the Japanese, it was a substantial cutback on game time considering they had long found aesthetic pleasure in slow-paced games. Back in the 1930s, one round easily lasted for three days as each player were given 13 hours.

What is the significance of time limit in Go? Longer time limit allows the player to gain deeper understanding of the situation on the Go board. There is more time to anticipate how a move would playout to effect change in the game. Players can benefit from long time limit by coming up with more efficient moves that can later spin off more strategically favorable moves. In Japan, Go was embraced as a form of art, a self-cultivating journey, and the beauty of it lied in hours of intense thinking to reach 'enlightenment'- or the most effective and the perfect move. This tradition of playing Go for long hours has been preserved in Japan, where it is played for 8 hours long when everything else in today's life moves apace.

By contrast, players depend on their experiences and intuition when playing quick games where the time limit is shorter. Despite years of training and experience, the probability of making mistakes is higher in quick games, hence the quality of the moves is more likely to be disappointing than games played over long hours.

I cannot say which is better because it is a matter of format. Competing with one's most meticulously thought moves over long hours is meaningful in its own way while playing by intuition is also meaningful in another way. A professional Go player must be well trained for both types of games.

One cannot rely on intuition alone, or skill to play Go. I encourage beginning or intermediate level players to play quick games because spending a lot of time on the moves do not necessarily guarantee optimal moves at those levels. I believe beginners should experiment with the first idea that comes to their mind. They may like it or regret it, but they will gradually get the feel of it and begin to read the implications of each move, and become more comfortable and familiar with the game. It is important to strike the balance between quick and slow games because they require skills that reinforce each other.

Recently, however, quick games have become the trend. The standard time limit in most local matches is 1 hour per player. There are also ultra-quick games that allow 20, 10 or even 5 minutes to each player. On the other hand, slow Go games played for 2-3 hours are harder to find these days. In the past, the ratio of slow games to quick ones used to be 80 to 20; this ratio has been reversed over the years.

I understand that quick games may be the inevitable trend. For those who are used to the head-spinning speed of computer games and the smartphones will find Go games that takes as long as 5 to 6 hours an unbearable drag. With the number of Go population on the decline, insisting to play only slow games may not be the wisest idea. Quick Go games can offer the same level of, or even more thrill and excitement than computer games. In this sense, there is a pull factor that can attract the younger generation to cultivate an interest in Go. Making quick games the mainstream, however, would be too risky because a sharp cut in the time limit is prone to compromised game quality. I will be blunt. Short games train the mind to develop depthless moves and shallow tricks. There is very little 'enlightenment' involved.

Underused skills are bound to degenerate. For the past decades, the game of Go has evolved through long hours of fierce thinking that gave birth to extraordinary styles; Go Seigen redefined the framework and the level of modern Go; Minoru Kitani created a new opening theory; Cho Chikun became the name for sharp and fierce moves; Lee Changho is indomitable in any crisis. It was those deep thought games that trained top-ranking players to perform at their best despite the time limit.

The reality is quite different today. Young professional players, conditioned to play quick games, cannot help themselves but collapse when engaged in long games. They have very little clue about how to maximize the time given to them as they have never spent so much time to mull over a move.

Dr. Bai Taeil at the Korea Baduk Association provides an explanation with his research. Dr. Bai, a physicist, tested the correlation between a player's skill and the length of games. He divided young professional players into two groups; one was good at quick games and the other in slow games. When the ranking of the two groups were compared against each other, results revealed that players with higher ranking in quick games peaked out in performance between the ages of 20 to 22. In contrast, the other group, who played longer games, showed slow progress in their early 20s but their breakthrough comes after the age of 25, as evident in their remarkable performance in international tournaments.

Dr. Bai believes the results of his study provide an explanation as to why Korean players have done poorly in recent international championships. Some international competitions have introduced the 1-hour time limit to keep up with the changes of the times. But the more prestigious international tournaments like the Ing Cup, the Chunlan Cup, and the Samsung Fire & Marine Insurance World Masters Baduk still apply the 2-3 hour time limit. Korean players used to win every championship cup until the early 2000s but that is not the case anymore. Players from China or Japan have performed far more remarkable. I am afraid Korean players also fall behind in terms of the quality of the game.

The pursuit of speed came with a price. Speed gives the pleasure, the thrill, and the excitement. But quick games have no place for vigilance and foresight. The habit of playing speedy games does not prepare one to think it through when caution is required. Instead, the disposition to rush through making a decision kicks in.

People have become too spontaneous often these days. They put feelings before reason and allow their emotions to be in charge of their behavior. They act on impulse and make mistakes they regret afterwards; for example, submitting their resignation at work immediately after criticized by their manager, saying harsh words to family and friends that hurt their feelings, lying to keep themselves out of trouble and getting caught lying. It is too late when damage is done. Even if one can undo it, it may take a long time and a lot of effort.

We live in the age of quick changes. I believe this is all the more reason to take things seriously and think thoroughly. Troubles and conflicts that happen around us could have been avoided if more thought was given before taking action. Time and again, individuals have lost candidacy for public office because of plagiarizing someone else's dissertation, politicians have made promises that cannot be fulfilled just to win the election, and celebrates have become the center of gossip because of careless comments made in public.

Masaki Takemiya 9P, who is famous for his 'cosmic style' of building houses in the center of the board, once spent as long as 5 hours and 7 minutes out of the 8-hour time limit given to him for a single move. Masaki stared at the board with a serious expression for 5 hours and 7 minutes. But why? Why did it take him 5 hours to place a single stone on the board?

Masaki knew that the position of a single stone could decide the outcome of the game. One careless move can cause strangulation or come back as a stab in the back when the game reaches the tipping point. On the other hand, one good move can make one the winner of the game.

How should we choose where to play in our lives? Life is long and to be successful in life, much thought has to be given to each move. Over time, one will be in control of one's thoughts and become capable of making optimal decisions even at the face of pressing issues. Those who play with fast hands have been incubated for tens of thousands of hours, training to think through their moves. Likewise, our mind can be turned into a faster powerful thinking tool with training.

Go Gods Can't Have Too Much Fun

In the game of Go, overtime counting begins when the main time is exhausted. For time control, tournaments use different overtime systems. For example, some give 5 overtime periods of 30 seconds each, some 1 period of 1 minute each. The overtime rules vary even more in international competitions, from no overtime period to 5 overtime periods of 40 minutes. The Ing Cup gives an extension of 35 minutes instead of an overtime and penalizes 2 points when the player has maxed out on the extra time. Every Go player has to play under the pressure of time.

A player must make a move before the overtime counting ends during each overtime period. When all of the allowable overtime periods are used up, the player can lose on time. In my heydays, I rarely played under time pressure because I always managed to make quick moves. I had so much left over time that some teased I could make a lot of money from selling it. But I myself had the experience of suffering a loss on time. By the mid-2000s, the Korea Baduk Association had replaced the timekeeper with a Go timer that was to be self-operated by the player. On several occasions, I forgot to press the button right after making my move, which resulted in my defeat on time. Unlike the younger players, older players like me embarrassed ourselves by making unbelievably ridiculous mistakes before we became comfortable using the timer clock.

I recall humiliating myself by losing on time. It happened twice in my entire career. I was mortified not because I was clumsy with the timer clock, but because I had used up all of my overtime chances and still clueless about what to do. It was bizarre. I remember hearing the time-keeper saying, "This is the last overtime counting. One, two, three...." I was supposed to put my stone when I heard the voice counting "... eight, nine, and ten", but I froze – I could not think nor even lift a finger and I could not explain why. The press blamed my age but inside, I knew that I had just given up the game then. There was no way a professional player could justify it.

Sometimes I wonder what it would be like playing Go without a time limit or overtime counting. But I shake my head sideways without giving it a second thought. A match must be fought within the given time. Without a time limit, no one would make a move until the best move comes to one's mind. It would literally take dozens of days to finish a game, turning it into a never-ending pastime of the immortal Gods and Goddesses. In fact, there was a time when the time limit was overgenerous in Japan. Until the 1930s, Go was an extremely slow-paced game. A case in point was the 1938 Honinbo Shusai versus Minoru Kitani game. Shusai was the 21st and the last heir to inherit the 'Honinbo' title of the Honinbo House, one of the major Go houses in Japan that survived until 1940. Shusai and Kitani were each given 40 hours but it took 158 days to finish one round as it was frequently disturbed by Shusai's poor health condition.

In Japan, a sealed move was used whenever the game went into recess. The next move to be made would be sealed in an envelope and played when the game resumes. The purpose of the sealed envelope is to ensure none of the players know the board position when it is their turn to make the next move. In this way, no one could take advantage of the adjournment. The Shusai vs Kitani match went on for 158 days during which the game adjourned for 15 times, hence 15 envelops sealed. Showing enormous amount of patience to the duration of the game is typical of Japan. The rationale for the tolerance was that Go was more than a strategic board game. It was a form of art and a way of seeking truth. But, Go Seigen, who also studied under Master Segoe and was a long-time Go companion of mine, thought otherwise. He had a visionary idea which was ahead of his time. Go Seigen believed in a drastic cutback in the time limit and prudence in practicing sealed envelope to ensure a fair level playing field.

The Shusai vs Kitani 158-day match, needless to say, was recorded as one of the most inspiring games in the history of Go in Japan. Shusai and Kitani had days to think of the next best moves whenever there was a call for a sealed envelope, on top of the generous default time limit. The Go board must have been embroidered with moves akin to the graceful works of the Gods. However, sometimes, as the proverb says, "a bad move is born from too much contemplation," awkward moves were made throwing the board position into disarray. Strokes of genius can also be observed in shorter games with 1 to 2 hours of time limit. However, the reasonable assumption is that it was the culmination of a long-term training and experience.

Time limit is necessary. Deadlines serve as a strong motivation for players to completely immerse themselves in the game. Besides, we only get to live for a finite period of life. In order to live a desirable life, the prerequisite is to make efficient use of the limited time one is granted.

Deadlines are also set up as a way of making a commitment. They must be kept for the society to function smoothly as a whole. An architect has to complete the construction within the period of contract, a factory owner must supply on the agreed date, and managers of an organization must put together a report or a plan by the deadline. Missed deadlines can trigger a chain of chaos on the part of various stakeholders. Anyone who aspires to become an expert must train and practice to complete tasks on time. On-time completion is a key part of professionalism.

To become a professional in the area of one's interest, one must experience the very important sense of achievement of meeting deadlines. In a way, schools prepare us for a fair play. One could perhaps take the classroom experience and apply it elsewhere, challenge oneself by personal goals. There is no need to be too tough on the deadlines in the beginning. Work around what works and take it from there. Goals can be stretched gradually depending on the type and nature of the projects one wishes to accomplish. Train oneself to manage time efficiently by taking on long-term and short-term assignments.

What is worse than exceeding the overtime is not being able to make up one's mind about the next move. A mediocre alternative is better than being hand-tied because the game must go on. Professional Go players have made a name of themselves with extraordinary game records which was only possible because they withstood the harsh training under the pressure of time. This is the essence of professionalism. Racing against time is the fate of every professional player. And to become a true professional, one must win the race.

FORESIGHT

Professional Go players attempt to anticipate as much as possible. Some can even read 50 or 100 moves ahead. They do not guess the position of every move. But they read the positions in a way unimaginable to the ordinary mind.

Professional Go players see images in their minds. The sequences and the order of the moves that will be played out come very natural to them, almost instantaneously. But it is not the obvious they are worried about. Rather, they are concerned about missing out on the unforeseen variables that could have an impact on their strategy. So they ponder the unexpected until cornered by the overtime counting asking themselves; how would my opponent react to my move and how should I counter back, which positions are worth keeping, and what options are there in the worst case scenario. Professional players compare all the options against every possible odds, visualizing what is yet to come. In this sense, it may be more accurate to refer to 'reading the moves' as 'perceiving the upcoming developments.'

Professional Go players decide how they wish to play the game in the very beginning. The planning and strategizing are already done in the early phase of the game. The rest of the game is spent on reducing the probability of variables associated with each stone placed on a specific position. The ultimate goal is to lead the flow of the game as planned.

In real life, we plan our moves. Every conversation, behavior at work, and buying and investing in a property are part of the big plan we have made for our lives. Anticipating is even necessary when one reports to the manager at work. One needs to decide whether to give a written or a verbal report, or present the outcome first, or go through the process first, because the way the reporting is done can affect the manager's reaction. Familiarizing oneself with the leadership style of the manager or knowing the manager's preference could be helpful in planning for the optimal way to report.

Anticipation becomes much more important to experts, especially, in professions such as real estate investors, stock brokers, and fund managers, whose job is to forecast the market. Most experts are skilled at understanding what is happening to the economic policy, consumer sentiment, price index, real estate market, and stock market in each country today. They are able to connect the dots to forecast the big picture; for example, the future of the world economy, consumer price movements, favorable areas of investment and the probable returns, in connection to each other.

The forecast may not always be accurate. Even exceptional experts, or a Go player 9P like myself can arrive in the wrong conclusion because of missing an important factor, but largely, because we are inclined to interpret things to our advantage. The urge to seek immediate gains can be misleading. Organizations and the society as a whole make the same mistake of interpreting to their favor and as a result, making the wrong decision. For instance, why were prominent economists unable to predict the 2008 global finance crisis in advance? Why did banks take the risk of providing mortgage loans to people with low credit rating? Worse, how could they even think of selling subprime mortgage-backed derivatives to investment banks?

The best a rotten apple can produce is a glass of rotten apple juice. It will still be the same rotten apple juice no matter how much sweetener or scent are added. An alarm should have gone off when those mortgage-backed financial assets were traded in the market to warn about their repercussions. Nevertheless, no one warned against the dangers of those assets. Blinded by immediate gains, no one did a thorough analysis of their impact on the economy. Everyone dismissed the flickering danger signal as they sought after short-term high return on their investment.

When one is blinded by immediate gains, one fails to foresee three or four moves ahead, compromising the positions on the board. A Go master never becomes too excited when a position that can bring immediate advantage comes into view. The opponent would have probably seen it too and must have already braced to take a counter action. Throwing oneself into what looks appealing now could result in a dire loss later. The more tempting it is, the greater the risk. It could be a bait which would cost one an arm and a leg.

Try to refrain from skimming over a situation. Look at the big picture. What one finds attractive, others may find attractive, too, which ironically, makes it less valuable. Furthermore, there must be someone out there going after what is more valuable with a bigger picture in mind. Try to see the forest and not just the tree while asking oneself if one is aligned with the direction one wishes to follow. Keep sight of the overall view and ride on the stream. The rest shall follow.

BATOO: THE WORTH OF A BAD MOVE

Online games were in full swing in Korea in 2009. And I too got a firsthand experience of this huge change that swept across the country. I found myself sitting in front of a computer wearing a headset to play some games on line. I have never played any other games but Go. I played 'Batoo,' short for 'Baduk (the Korean term for Go) Jentoo,' or Baduk Battle. 'Batoo' was an online board game built on the offline Go. It had similar rules with Go, but as its name suggests, included more exciting combat-style factors.

People became concerned when I, "a respected National Hand," according to them, became attracted to online games which seemed to be intended for young people.

"It's ungraceful of a National Hand to play online games."

"He is crazy about making money."

"He is trying to make up for his poor performance in Go."

I received more than enough disapproval and accusations, but I had my own reasons. I did not know how others saw it, but it was not anything close to a spur-of-the moment decision to play online. I had thought about it seriously and give it a try to look ahead, although it may have been a bad move.

Less people were playing Go in Korea and Korean players who had gone from strength to strength were on the verge of being outperformed by Chinese players. There were more entertainment choices outside the household and even more exciting online games penetrating every household, resulting in Go losing ground. The future of Go depended on the young generation but they were losing interest in the game. There seemed to be very little that could be done about the trend. I thought the game of Go should reach out to the young people if they no longer came to play Go.

I assumed that those who liked Batoo would be interested in Go as well because the online game was rooted in the Go. The basic rule of capturing the opponent's stones to expand territories by building houses was the same, except that 'Batoo' had some special rules and gambling elements to it that allowed beginners to develop strategies to beat a Go player 9P. Another appealing aspect of 'Batoo' was the World Batoo League which awarded a total prize money of 1.2 billion won in a year.

I became involved in Batoo hoping that this fun game would appeal to the young and eventually make them being interested in Go. I was engaged from the beginning to provide advice on the development of the game and played in the World Batoo League with junior players. I had interviews with various media outlets to promote the game. I allowed myself to be the face of this novel game and the wingman. I did not mind being crushed when playing games with those who were far younger than I was.

Many were apprehensive and disapproving of my involvement in promoting Batoo. They felt Batoo was damaging the reputation of Go, let alone attracting more people, and eventually drive people away from playing Go. They had a valid concern, but we could not afford to cling on to the reputation of Go because the world had moved on. When in Rome, do as the Romans do. When in a swimming pool, swimsuits must be worn. The world was a different place and we had to change accordingly.

Batoo may have caused damage to the reputation of Go, but it could not have caused any further decline in the number of people playing Go. Batoo was only one of many online games. No matter how much fun Batoo was, people were eventually going to return to play the authentic strategy board game of Go which had survived for more than 4,000 years. Batoo could not have possibly posed any threat to the authority of Go. Even if it did, it would have been a light jab, at most. Go would still have been invincible. I was determined to promote the on-line spin-off of Go in the hope of redirecting the crowd to the ancient game and reviving its popularity. It was not an impulsive decision and I had thought everything through. I knew that there would be criticisms. I knew that Batoo may not take off. I also knew that the failure would reflect negatively on my reputation as the National Hand. Nevertheless, I was not afraid of scandalizing the Go community. Rather, it was liberating to act on my personal conviction. Someone in the Go community had to do it. I believed I was in the best position to take the risk considering my age and reputation. The pressure and the responsibility would have been too much if someone younger or older than me took the risks associated with Batoo.

Being involved in Batoo turned out to be a bad move for me. A bad move is a move that is against the interest of a player. Professional players work hard to avoid bad moves because they can tip the entire game to the disadvantage of the player in the blink of an eye. Victory is reserved for those who avoid making a bad move, not those who make a move akin to the stroke of a genius. In the real world, however, one may be forced to make a bad move with knowledge that it may bring more harm than good because of circumstantial issues, or to stick to one's principles.

I believe in the evolution of Go. I am willing to take a blow to my reputation if that is what it takes to move Go forward. There are people who join labor or civic movements for a social cause without expecting any personal gains. Some are devoted to things that do not promise them financial benefits nor public recognition. But standing by one's principles makes the soul feel liberated.

Unfortunately, Batoo was not successful. It had to shut down its service and my vision to expand the foundation of Go perished with Batoo.

Some may have sneered, "Hunhyun, it serves you right!" But I don't think it was wrong to support Batoo. Batoo failed, but it was worth trying. Just because the outcome was not something one had in mind doesn't mean it was a bad idea.

I am still looking for an effective way to promote Go. I have worked hard with the hope of including Go in the next Summer Olympics as well as at the National Sports Festival, a nation-wide sports event held in every autumn in Korea. I am ready to take my chances, including making another bad move, to promote Go and make way for its evolution.

THE THREE COLOR RAINBOW

There was an interesting show about the colors of a rainbow on television. Koreans are taught that a rainbow has seven colors. But I found out this standard is taught only in a few countries, including Korea. In the U.S., the 'official' number of colors of a rainbow is seven, but most Americans believed a rainbow had six colors, as most Europeans did. In Ancient Maya, the colors of the rainbow were classified into five according to historical records. This finding reminded me of how the older generation in Korea refer to the rainbow as a 'five-colored rainbow.' Those who are taught that a rainbow has five colors could actually see only five colors in a rainbow. The shade of orange between red and yellow, or the difference between navy and purple, hardly meant anything to them. If

141

one is taught the rainbow has three colors, the visible spectrum of colors is bound to be simplified into those three colors, leaving very little room to explore what is beyond.

In fact, a computer-generated color analysis of a rainbow shows that it has tens of thousands of shades. Although they may not all be distinguishable by the human eyes, we may still be able to tell that there are more than seven colors in a rainbow. However, the moment one is taught a rainbow has seven colors in school, one no longer makes the effort to inquire about the colors of the rainbow. When it comes to skills, one stops challenging oneself to hone the skills necessary to move on to the next level believing that one has already mastered it all.

That is when things start to go wrong. We believe we know everything and that we had thought through every option before making a choice. However, this is a serious delusion, simply because no one has the capability to know everything. It happens in Go competitions. One misinterprets the situation on the Go board because of an unanticipated variable. But the more one trains to play Go, more knowledge is accumulated, hence one becomes progressively better at reading the positions. Intuition and experience are important but one has to have a wider scope of knowledge. One must continue to learn to be able to read the position on the board from different perspectives.

For this reason, learning must go on. Reading text books on Go, analyzing game records, and solving as many life-and-death problems in Go must continue for a professional player to sharpen the game skills. Learning, in the broader sense, could include collecting information and building knowledge in one's relevant field, and to keep oneself excited about what is happening around the world.

The game of Go is a miniature of our life. But professional Go players tend to be cut off from the real world. Background knowledge in history, culture, or the society is not required to play the game. One can be the best in Go without having the slightest idea of the rest of the world. Master Segoe had no idea how much a sack of potato cost or which route the buses in his neighborhood took all his life. Now that I have slowed down on building my career, I have started to watch the news and dramas on the T.V., but I did not have a clue on what was happening in politics and the economy at the height of my career. I did not even have enough time to just practice Go. If I had any spare time, I preferred to use it to solve one more life-and-death problem to deepen my knowledge of Go. I believe I was not the only Go player who chose to train oneself in seclusion. Most professional players are geniuses when they are playing Go; but one may be surprised to find out that they have very little practical knowledge of how to get by in the real world.

Unlike professional Go, most jobs are closely linked to what happens day-to-day in the real world; a good writer chooses a topic that the public can relate to; a good songwriter creates a melody that can appeal to the taste of the masses; a doctor has to be an effective communicator to work with the patients; and the competitive edge of an IT person lies in keeping oneself up-to-date with the latest technology and their application in everyday life.

To anticipate the events of our lives, building expertise in one's field must continue while keeping abreast with what's happening in the world. We need to be open to different topics. Knowledge and information acquired must be stored in the mind like a database. Those pieces of information may seem irrelevant to one's job today, if accumulated over time, evolve into a system of knowledge and experience that help make an informed decision on the next-steps of life.

The humanities have an important role to play here. They serve as a framework to gain in-depth understanding of the world and humanity. We get to trace the footprint of mankind in history, philosophy, science, and the arts and look at the world and our future with a wider perspective. When we put things into perspective, preludes to larger events become visible, giving insight and moving us to prepare for what is to unfold.

Anxiety stems from limited knowledge and information. As the saying goes, knowledge is power. Those who are well-informed can minimize making mistakes and anticipate further. One must work hard to gain knowledge and improve skills. Stay excited about learning and open to different areas. Being well-informed is the best strategy to anticipate the variables that can impact one's life.

"Replaying the game after winning is a winning habit;
reviewing the game after losing it prepares one to win the next game."

Chapter 6

Masters' Ways to Self-Heal

FACE YOUR MISTAKES

The winner of the 2014 Guksu Title Match was going to be decided be-tween Cho Hanseung 9P and Lee Sedol. Hanseung was a gold medalist in the men's Go team event in the 2010 at the 16th Guangzhou Asian Games. Sedol lost the first two rounds to Hanseung. But I was very impressed by Sedol during the game review.

A game review literally means the player 'replays' the game. In profes-sional Go, however, it is rare to go through every single move. It is even more so in longer games because both the winner and the loser are too ex-hausted to replay the game after being engaged in a 2-3 hour nerve-brak-ing brain battle. Game reviews become a huge burden. Instead of a game review, the players usually give a brief overview about what went well for the winner, what the loser missed, and the move that decided the outcome of the game.

Hanseung and Sedol's game review, however, did not turn out to be business as usual at all. Sedol poured questions at Hanseung as he kept picking up the stones and placing them around the grids. The seasoned timekeeper, who was quick to foresee that the session was going to stretch over his duty hours, happily left giving them all the time they needed. It took Sedol and Hanseung another hour and a half after the timekeeper left to go over their game. Not only that, the review evolved into a full-scale discussion as others joined in to give their analysis of the game. The review paid off when a few days later, Sedol won the third round after blitzing Hanseung. Although Hanseung won the championship in the end, the way Sedol got right on to face the causes of his defeat in the second round and quickly applying the lessons to outscore Hanseung in the following round ought to be highly commended and applauded.

At the 3rd Tongyang Securities Cup held in 1991, Rin Kaiho 9P lost to Changho when the game took a dramatic turn to Changho's favor despite Rin Kaiho's predominance throughout the match. But Rin Kaiho was a true Go master both in terms of skills and character. Rin Kaiho did not reveal a single tinge of resentment against his 17-year old opponent who took away the world champion title before his very eyes. Instead, he sat down with Changho and took the time to review the game. Ever since that day, Rin Kaiho became Changho's most admired person.

Game reviews may come across as extraordinary or even sentimental to those outside the Go community. How is it even possible to have the winner and the loser sit face-to-face to go over a game they had just finished playing? It seems like the dignified way of closing the match. For the Go players, it is both professional courtesy to agree to a game review as well as the most efficient way to learn why the game was lost or won.

Anyone who loses must find out the reason of defeat one way or another. The easiest way would be to ask the opponent sitting across the board than trying to figure it out alone at home. Having said that, reviewing immediately after a game may not be easy at all when the game itself is arduous most of the time. It becomes harder to endure, particularly, when one has been defeated. One feels torn apart as one tries to process powerful emotions such as anger and disappointment. Imagine having to repress one's emotions and sit through an entire review. It is painful indeed as if someone is rubbing salt on one's wound. The loser of the game may appear calm but inside one is suffering.

A professional player who has just been defeated experiences mental chaos despite appearing confident and composed. At the 2001 LG Cup World Baduk Championship, Sedol finished second place after losing to Changho three rounds in a row in the final match. He had, in fact, won the first two. The 17-year-old Sedol showed incredible self-control during the game review, but he was said to have cried buckets for a long time when he got home. From time to time, we come across players who decline game reviews and are in such a rush to get home. The audience may think they lack professional courtesy. But, in reality, they may be rushing to a washroom because they cannot hold back their tears.

I have never actually cried but I wanted to cry so many times. I have come to care less about winning or losing. I am just grateful that I can still play Go. But I hated losing when I was young. I was in desperate need to be alone after I managed to finish the review of the game I had just lost. I did not know how to comfort myself. I did not drink nor have any hobbies. The only thing I could do was to take a long walk all night until I was exhausted and had to walk back home. I did not let anyone see me when I was completely shaken up, not even my wife who was the closest person to me.

The paradox is that neither the winner of the game feels comfortable about game reviews. The relationship the winner has with the opponent complicates the situation, not to mention having to demonstrate professional courtesy as well by restraining from expressing joy. Back in the days when Changho took every single title I had, even the audience felt uneasy and nervous during our game reviews. Changho, feeling guilty about defeating me, his teacher, could not bring himself to look at me or to answer my questions.

Reviewing a game is a torture for both the winner and the loser of the game. But the review sessions must carry on. It is the only way to be sure of what went right and what went wrong. Doing a thorough review allows players to avoid repeating the same mistakes and help them discover better moves for the next games. In the world of competitive Go, reviewing games is the basic requirement. It helps winners develop winning habits, and prepares those defeated for a victory.

How would one feel, if one has to revisit one's mistakes over and over? Anyone would choose to avoid doing it in the first place, if possible. No one enjoys looking at their weaknesses. But a fighter must look hard at them. The only way to win is to admit one's mistakes and to never repeat them. A fighter should know better than to ignore one's weaknesses.

Making a routine out of reviewing is not limited to Go or competitive sports. Everyone reviews or replays at different levels. One thinks about how the day went by lying on the bed at the end of the day; one may regret or do a self-reflection of some of the events that took place during the day, such as being criticized by the manager, being commended for an achievement, how the meeting went in the office, or how the project is making progress. Whatever it is that one regrets, one should not avoid it. Some make the attempt to forget embarrassing or regretful moments. Some chose to justify their mistakes or blame them on others. It is not about how quickly one gets over failure, but how one overcomes it. One needs to have a clear diagnosis of what went wrong instead of pointing fingers at others or denying anything ever happened. In real life, revisiting mistakes prevents one from repeating them. The value of it lies in giving oneself the quiet time for self-reflection and address personal issues.

One needs to look at one's weaknesses squarely even if it is painful. The more painful it is, the closer one has to look at it. A mistake is never made by coincidence. It is made by immaturity and inexperience. Refusing to accept responsibility and fix the problem is an immature behavior.

Admit to making a mistake. Face one's mistakes squarely and honestly. Review one's game every day, no matter how painful it is. One will grow professionally and become a mature adult.

Enemies are the Greatest Teachers

Reviewing a game is necessary to explore the roads not taken after the actual game has taken place. Professional Go players get to think about possible variations of their moves and positions. What if I had chosen to put this stone at this place instead of the other one? Would it have made all the difference in the outcome?

The sore loser can anxiously try to 'win' the review and let out the frustration. On the other hand, the winner tends to be easy-going and will try to let the opponent win the review. The winner offers consolation and encouragement to the opponent; "I could have lost if you had made that move," or, "there is no way I could have escaped that." But, in some cases, game reviews can be as tight as the actual game, for example, when the defeated individual comes up with an idea that can turn the game around, and the opponent replies with a powerful move that equals it out. This dynamic can trigger an exhaustive debate and time-consuming review that lasts longer than the actual game.

Reviewing a game is important because it is a window to the opponent's way of thinking. The two players have the opportunity to learn new, unique ideas from each other and exchange feedback. In this respect, game reviews can be a paradigm-shifting experience for some. Anyone who has had an amazing mind-blowing experience will know what I mean. An old framework of thinking is smashed into pieces and the mind feels as if it has been drilled through. The sheer shock of it leaves one feeling bewildered. But when the shock is absorbed and the dust settles, one begins to think at a whole different level. Embracing other people's system of thinking therefore has the power to revolutionize one's own system. This is all the more reason to stay open-minded, in particular, about the opponent. Time and again, game reviews have demonstrated that players have much to offer to each other. The opponent can be a 'great teacher' for those who are open to their input and appreciate their commentaries. It would be a shame to treat the opponent as hostile and let jealousy and the sense of rivalry get in the way of learning.

Nobody likes being defeated or asking for help on bended knees. But anybody who wants to win must be willing to bow one's head to the winner and ask for a lesson. One must inquire as much as possible and learn how to incorporate the winner's way of thinking into one's own style.

Collective knowledge sharing and the culture of open discussion have been the two important drivers of Go's continued success. The Go game record books are akin to the open-source programs on the Internet accessible to anyone and open to improvements. Every day, comments about the game records of top-ranking players fill up the message boards on Go-related websites. This common space welcomes anyone with new ideas. Go, being a sport for players of all age, gender and ranks, nurtures open and interactive dynamics.

In 1997, I was flying to Japan with other professional players to participate in the 10th Fujistu Cup World Go Championship. I was revisiting the second round of the final match that I played against Satoru Kobayashi at the 8th Tongyang Securities Cup which was held a few days ago. I had won the game but I was not quite satisfied with how I played it. Jimmy Cha, who was sitting beside me, brought up the topic so I shared with him what was on my mind.

"In hindsight, there was a better way to win. I could have ended the game earlier, but I chose the less optimal opening move." Changho, who was sitting behind us overheard our conversation. As soon as he unpacked at the hotel, he sat down and started to think of any counter-response to the move I regretted not making. When Changho finally came up with one that night, he shared it with his peer, Choi Myunghoon 5P (now 9P).

"Do you remember the move Mr. Cho mentioned on the plane? It would not have worked because there is a countermove."

Myunghoon relayed it to Jimmy, who, in turn, passed the message to me. That night, I stayed up thinking about how to reply to the counter-move.

"Do you remember the move Changho came up with yesterday? What would he do if I fend off his move with this one?"

Jimmy slapped his knee and exclaimed.

"He will be captured!"

We never stop reviewing games. Chances are someone is trying to find another clever response as we speak now. We will learn the moves others invented and try to discover other countermoves through never-ending game reviews. Hence the on-going evolution of Go.

REPLAY, EVERYDAY

A long time ago, I had a visitor who came looking for me to a Go club. As soon as he finished introducing himself, he blurted out.

"I can beat you, Mr. Cho!"

"I beg your pardon?"

"I have replayed your games for hundreds of times. As the old saying goes, if you know your enemy and yourself, you can win every battle. Mr. Cho, you don't know me, but I know your games like the back of my hand. So, I can beat you!"

I did not know how to reply other than saying, "Oh, you think so?" The short conversation ended there.

Studying game records is a prerequisite for learning to play Go. Beginners and professionals alike, everyone needs to study game records to improve their skills. Records of past games that have become famous worldwide classics, major championship games, games played between top professional players must be studied. Replaying someone else's game literally involves placing all the stones in the order written in the game record. The process is similar to reviewing one's own game, except one is reconstructing someone else's game. In this way, players get to learn how the masters think and understand the logic behind each move; the opening strategies, patterns and crisis management skills. Beginners can see their skills dramatically improve in a short period of time just by analyzing the game records.

Another reason to replay the game records is to identify any possible mistakes. Every game record has a weak link, even the great ones. Whether it be an honest mistake, a careless mistake, or mistakes that made or break the game, it may take up to a few dozens of days to go through one game record. It would have been nice if reviewing someone else's game can teach you everything about the person, but unfortunately, it does not.

Game records reflect the player's style; they help to understand whether the player prefers to play offense or is meticulous. The most one can get out of game records is getting a sense of the style of the player. This is because masters in Go can switch their gear at any moment as they see fit. They can shift to playing defense from their usual offensive style. They can be versatile depending on the situation on the board. It is impossible to know the masters' style and plays inside out from simply memorizing the game records.

Of all the strategy board games, Go has the largest number of outcomes. With simple mathematics, one loses track attempting to count them because the number of cases come out to a seven-hundred digit number. The number of outcomes may show a sharp drop if the rules of different Go competitions are applied to filter the cases. However, there are too many outcomes remaining to keep track of. Different rules of the game and the creativity of the players combine, rendering it possible to produce a few hundred million or trillion combinations of outcomes. One game can also be mapped out in thousands of different ways depending on where the players decide to place their first stones. Game records have been recorded for over two centuries but not a single case of identical records was found. This provides explanation to why Artificial Intelligence is catching up with human intelligence only now to play Go games, whereas relatively speaking, sophisticated computer programming was not required to win human intelligence in chess games.

I used to scour my opponent's game records with full attention before the actual game in the hope of finding out about my counterpart's style. But I soon realized that studying my opponent's game did not help me much. It was not worth putting a strategy together based on those game records because it only took one unexpected move from the opponent to shift the flow of the game entirely. Building a strategy that can respond to every single variable would take forever, needless to say, absurd. It made more sense to work on my reading rather than spending too much time analyzing my counterpart.

The best way to train is to replay the game on the same day every day. One needs to remember the game played earlier in the day and try to reconstruct it. Replaying gives up-to-date insight to the overall level of the player. Any bad habits or practices must be fixed right away.

Master Segoe was not the kind who gave attention to every little detail when he was teaching his student. But he was very strict about replaying one's own game every day. Reviewing the game played earlier during the day after dinner was an important part of my daily routine. Master Segoe would watch me reviewing my own game and sometimes pointed his finger at a stone. He did not make any facial expression nor did he say anything, but I knew that that was the stone I had to think over.

Master Segoe's way of teaching was not so different from how I taught Changho. Diligence was already his middle name when Changho came to study under me. We let Changho stay in a room where all the books on Go were stored. Changho read every single one of them while he lived with us and had read and analyzed every book on game records.

Sometimes I asked Changho to replay his game in my presence. Strangely enough, he was unable to remember his game. After placing a few stones on the board, he sat like a stone, saying that he could not remember the positions of the rest of the stones. It came as a surprise because most professional players did not need any special effort to re-member their own games and were able to remember others' records at a glance. I asked Changho to do one thing. "Try to remember the game you played that day. It will help you understand your mistakes and how to fix them."

Ever since that day, Changho made a lot of effort to remember his games. He seemed a little slow in the beginning but with regular practice, he succeeded in recalling his moves. It has been a while since Changho stepped down from the 'throne.' Nevertheless, he still spends a lot of time replaying his games and reviewing others' game records, day and night. When his opponents ask Changho to review games with them, he offers analysis in great detail and with respect to his opponents. He is open to sharing his strategy without any reservation with those who ask for his insight. Chagnho has gained popularity, particularly in China, where Go fans appreciate his modest and benevolent attitude toward game reviews.

In 2004, Changho was taking a rest at a hotel after winning a close match against Hu Yaoyu 7P (now 8P) at the 5th Chunlan Cup World Professional Weiqi Championship. Hu Yaoyu showed up without notice at Changho's room door with a group of young players repeatedly asking for a game review. Changho received them with a warm greeting. He willingly went over the game with them, answering all of their questions until dawn while rubbing his sleepy eyes. It was essentially his sincerity that took him to the 'throne,' and kept him respected even when he stepped down from it.

ADMIT DEFEAT AND MOVE ON

There are moments I want to tear my hair out while replaying my own games. Self-reproach becomes unbearable particularly after losing at a high-profile competition by a narrow margin. I continue to beat myself up over the lost game, asking myself how I could have possibly misread the positions, or if I did not have the intelligence to catch the hints. Dwelling on these emotions, however, holds me back from doing a proper game review, which is possible only when I can be objective about my own game. Without being free from the feelings of self-blame, regret, and being wrongfully defeated, game reviews could be misused to harass myself rather than to learn from revisiting my mistakes.

Most professional players including myself try very hard to shake off all the negative emotions and to focus on the game review itself, which is much easier said than done. It takes a while to let go the strong emotions experienced during a tight game, but most players are forced to jump right into a review session without having a moment to cool down. They eventually get used to the process. More accurately, they become used to the distress rather than getting better in controlling their emotions.

Sometimes the feeling of distress can last even long after the match is over. This is not a good sign. Prolonged self-blame can lead to self-doubt, hence a harbinger of a long slump. To professional players, game reviews mean more than review sessions. They are rituals we go through to overcome and flush out all the negative emotions. After a tough day, we can tell ourselves, 'I messed up the game today and that is done.' Stones once placed on the board cannot be taken back. When the game is over, all there is left to do is to learn my lesson and move on.

Humans tend to remember negative memories longer than positive ones. We tend to be quick at forgetting our success or commendations for our achievement. But we remember failures and embarrassing moments for a long time. Perhaps, it is because negative events give greater shock and far-reaching psychological repercussions. I am not free from this disposition. I had won 1,900 rounds of games out of 2,700, but the ones I remember are the lost games. I am not saying that I do not have memories from the prestigious championships, such as the Ing Cup and the Fujistu Cup which I won. I do have vivid memories of those moments. But, in terms of intensity, nothing compares to the memory of the Kisung Title Match which I lost by half a point to Changho.

I won the first two rounds of the final match at the 7th Kisung Title Match. But Changho caught up, winning the next two rounds. The score was a tie, 2:2, but Changho defeated me in the fifth and the final round by half a point. Many things were at stake; not to mention the huge prize money, the trophy, and the right to advance to the final as the title holder the following year. And I lost by half a point. No words could express my feelings at the time. Although it is natural to feel depressed when one loses a game, the sadness becomes even more unbearable when one loses by a narrow margin. The futility kept me awake all night. The mind and the body were exhausted but I was still tense from the game. So I tossed and turned, disturbing my wife's sleep, too.

Negative feelings must be put aside as soon as possible. I gain nothing from agonizing over my defeat for an extended period of time. Soon, there will be another competition in which I will have to participate. I turned to replaying my game over and over again. I felt free once I figured out what went wrong and what could have been done to win the game. 'Ah, that was my mistake. I could have won if I had done something else instead. I should not make the same mistake in the next game.' Game reviews gave me a sense of closure. And I felt better.

Talking to people can also help to overcome the negative emotions and that was exactly what I did after the Kisung Title Match. I shared the result of my game review with others and explained in detail why I had lost. I had shared it frequently enough that I started to look at my game record with more objectivity.

My experience of being a commentator at a few major competitions has helped me to let go of the bitter feelings. Watching the games as a commentator has allowed me to look at the games in a different way and accept that games are not just about winning. Go games are nerve-racking to the players, but exciting for the fans to watch. From the historical point-of-view, it is at these games that new game records are created. My role as the commentator gave me the distance to observe how emotions can run high during the game, only to quickly diminish when the game is over. I realized that all competitions, whether they make me smile or cry, are only ephemeral moments.

Imagining how my opponent must have felt after losing to me helped me get through the feelings of disappointment after I lost a game. I would prefer to win all the time but then my opponent would always be miserable, and the fans at the game would be bored. Where is the excitement in winning all the time, or in a life where everything goes as planned? It is the hardships that make one appreciate happiness; failures make success meaningful. It is rather assuring to think that winning and losing comes in cycles. Neither is permanent.

The sooner one overcomes a failure, the better it is. There is no time to waste on regretting past mistakes. Tomorrow is another day. Time should be spent wisely, perhaps going over one more game record rather than feeling depressed. One should not dwell on poor test results or job interviews that went wrong. The sky will not fall because one gets reprimanded at work. One needs to prepare oneself for the next opportunity, which will come very soon.

The purpose of review sessions is to create new strategies rather than to dwell over the mistakes. It is an opportunity to identify the causes of failure, for self-reflection, and to equip oneself with more creative and new ideas. One needs to find a way of letting disappointments go that works best for oneself and regain self-confidence as soon as possible. It would be lamentable to have the past anchor one down and keep one from moving forward.

"Sharing and offering favors are never one-way.
We are merely paying forward the generosity others have shown to us
and making an investment for a shared future."

Chapter 7

Think
Beyond

SHARING AND GIVING

Countries perceived to have the strongest cultural ties to the game of Go are somewhat still limited to Korea, China, and Japan. These three countries have the largest number of people playing the game, stand out in terms of the frequency and size of professional leagues and competitions. Above all, their players have far outperformed other nationalities in international competitions that there seems to be none who are at par with these countries.

But Go has actually grown out of the Korea-China-Japan tripartite zone. Taiwan is a Go success story outside the tripartite zone. Taiwan's only natural shortcoming is its small number of top-level players inevitably because of its relatively small number of population. But the impetus to popularize Go is there. The country knows how to organize professional competitions with vigor. It has also invested heavily in nurturing world-class players by sending its talented people to Japan to study Go. Rin Kai-ho, who ruled in Japan before Cho Chikun came along, is Taiwan-borne. Chen Shien, the undisputed leader of Go for a decade in Taiwan, learned to play the game at the Gwon Gapyong's Go school, the cradle of professional players in Korea, including the famous Lee Sedol and Choi Cheolhan. But, more than anyone else, it is Ing Changki, the Taiwanese billionaire who has contributed to build the ecosystem propitious to scaling up the size of the market and competitions. Without the Ing Cup that bears his name to honor his unselfish contribution of 400,000 dollars in prize money, there would be no Fujistu Cup. And without these two important championships, Go would not have gone global so soon. In this sense, Taiwan is a small giant in the history of Go in Asia. Outside East Asia, the number of people playing Go decreases sharply. Nevertheless, Go aficionados do exist and can be found around the world. The International Go Federation has 74 country members; 37 in Europe, 15 in the Americas, and 3 in Africa. The number of Go players in the U.S. is estimated to be 200,000, followed by 100,000 in Russia. Germany, the U.K., France, and the Netherlands each has 30,000 to 50,000 Go fans. In other words, there are 38 million people playing Go around the world. Although they are outnumbered by people who play chess, 600 million, it means something.

Full-scale globalization of Go owes much to Japan. Nihon Ki-in published the English Go magazine in the 1960s, the 'Go Review,' for the Go fans in the western hemisphere. Go centers were set up in the U.S., Europe, and South America and Go instructors were dispatched by none other but Japan. As such, the game became known in the west by its Japanese term, 'Go,' instead of the Korean term 'Baduk,' or the Chinese 'Weiqi.' As such, it was natural that Japanese became the language of Go.

Korea's impressive track record of outdoing Japan in many international competitions and its subsequent rise as a Go powerhouse makes it all the more prepared to take the initiative to promote playing Go around the world. Although the scale of its endeavors remain small, Korea has recently dispatched professional players as instructors to many European countries as well as the U.S., Australia, and Singapore. Volunteers, like Han Sangdae, professor of Go Studies at Myongji University in Korea, and former professor of Korean Studies at the University of Sydney, offer Go classes in English for the expatriate community in Korea and teach English to Go instructors before they leave for their overseas assignment. The Korea Amateur Go Association and the Korea Baduk Association have also raised funds to give financial support to the Go instructors who were dispatched overseas.

One might wonder why Korea, Japan and China care so much about making Go a globally popular game. There is only one reason. The more people play Go, the more competitions are held, and the more related market will expand. The globalization of Go can contribute to the development of relevant industries, which, in turn, will create more jobs. If growth picks up momentum and Go becomes widely played in Europe, North America, Latin America, and Africa, one day Go may become an official Olympic sport. The shared-vision is to see Go become the next 'chess.'

No country can achieve this aspiration alone. Japan provided the impetus to push both amateur and professional Go forward in Korea and

China, and the rise of Korea as a new strong player worked as an incentive to Japan and China to strive for more. Friendly mutual exchanges and the sense of healthy competition in the trilateral relationship must continue for the three to achieve collective growth and enjoy win-win outcomes. China, as the country of origin, Japan, as the birth place of the modern Go, and Korea, as the new player, can collectively reach out to countries that want to learn Go and offer them the benefits of the game.

Globalization of Go has seen a slow but passionate progress. The World Amateur Go Championship, an annual competition for amateur players, has had 50 to 60 players every year, who are willing to pay out of their own pocket to participate in the tournament. Their nationalities are also becoming more diverse, ranging from European nationalities to Vietnam, Brazil, India, and the Azerbaijani Republic. In addition, 500 to 700 Go aficionados play at the European Go Congress, an open competition for all amateurs and professionals, and their performance has progressively improved every year.

According to Professor Han, who also served as the chairperson of the Australian Go Association, there are a few Go enthusiasts in Australia who takes their passion for the game to the next level. A professor who taught French in university loved Go so much that he learned Japanese to become a professor of Japanese as well. His devotion for Go did not end there. Curious to learn the Korean approach to the game, he taught himself Korean and registered himself in the Gwon Gapyong's Go school in Korea. He lodged in Jongno, downtown Seoul and went every day to

Tapgol Park where he found senior citizens to play Go with. He did not care how the elderly locals in the park looked at him. He was very happy as long as he could play Go all day. Perhaps, he was lucky to learn some real life Go from the grandfathers who cheerfully agreed to play with him at the park whose names are not known to us.

Another Australian Go enthusiast, a PhD of Oriental studies who decided write a master's thesis on Go out of his love for the game. One day, two decades ago, he bought a big ranch in Tasmania, Australia. He put out an ad to hire ranch workers and one of the conditions was to play Go about two hours after work. Everyone who worked on his ranch came to enjoy playing the game and one of them even went as far as becoming 2K and later advanced into an international Go competition as an Australian youth representative. Years later, this eccentric ranch owner sold his ranch and moved to another city where he taught children in the town how to play Go. He put prize money of 2 dollars per game to make it interesting for the children and his strategy worked.

It is human nature to want to share something good. We recommend good movies, good music, and good books to our friends because we want to share the joy that comes from experiencing them. If a Go enthusiast can invite close friends to experience Go, and they refer the game to other people in their network, we can hope for the number of people playing Go to increase.

Building the infrastructure to enjoy the game must go hand in hand with recommending the game. There is a need for more Go centers or classes, Go text books for free distribution, and more instructors. I believe those who have benefited from the game must be mandated to lay the ground work to build the infrastructure and the environment propitious for learning Go. The pay-it-forward approach will create the virtuous cycle of rewarding those who are part of the Go network.

And it can do more beyond the Go network. I am a firm believer in sharing and rewarding those who shared with more returns, whether it be in psychological or material sense. Even if the reward is not directed to those who have given, someone in the chain is bound to have received it in the form of benevolence. In this way, the pay-it-forward approach can drive the society closer to our desirable model where the action of sharing is emulated and rewarded. Sharing and offering favors are never one-way. We are merely paying forward the generosity others have shown to us and making an investment for a shared future.

SHORT 'FRIENDSHIP', LONG-LASTING RIPPLE EFFECT

The year 2013 was marked by a seismic shift in the balance of 'Go' power between Korea, Japan, and China; in 7 international competitions, China swept away 6 trophies, and Japan took 1. For the first time in 17 years, Korea failed to win a single trophy from an international competition, which, to the eyes of many observers in the Go community, was an indication of the ever-deepening crisis Korea was facing.

By contrast, China was riding on the upward trend. Unlike Korea and Japan where the number of people playing Go was on a downward spiral, China was seeing the number of its Go population on a continuous rise. Increased funding and investment from the government and businesses stimulated the growth of professional leagues and China hosted one major international competition after another. It was also in 2013 that China overtook Korea in the total amount of prize money offered for all international competitions hosted by Chinese organizations and companies. Until 2013, Korea had offered the largest pool of prize money of 800 million won for three major international competitions combined; the Samsung Fire & Marine Insurance World Masters Baduk, the LG Cup World Baduk Championship, and the Nongshim Cup. But, that year, China increased its pool of prize money to 900 million won when it decided to host two more global competitions, the Shugo Cup and the Mlily Yumeyuri Cup World Championship.

Another new development was the generational change in professional Go that was taking place quickly. By the end of 2012, Lee Sedol ranked 1st, while Park Jeonghwan and Choi Cheolhan each ranked 6th and 7th in official world Go ranking. Both were much younger than Sedol. But, in 2015, Sedol ranked 5th when Jeonghwan rose to 2nd, and Kim Jiseok and Cheolhan, ranked 3rd and 8th, respectively. One may think that having 4 Korean players in the world top 10 should be good enough, but it was not. The prevalence of Chinese players in the world top 10 was something to be worried about. Shi Yue 9P ranked 1st, while Chen Yaoye, Mi Yuting, Gu Li, Zhou Ruiyang, and Tang Weixing also topped the chart. There were even more Chinese players below the top 10. It was imperative to notice that top-ranking players, except for Gu Li, were in their late teens or early 20s with a bright future ahead of them.

The Korean Go community took China's growth spurt very seriously. It was worried about the future of Korean Go. Japanese Go had been on a downhill trend ever since Korea took over its place as world champion. Korea was concerned its leadership in world Go could be on the same downward path. The Korean Go is in a crisis because it has lost the momentum. But I feel we need to look at the disintegration of its leadership with a different perspective.

Korea had dominated world Go for almost two decades. It could be time to handover the position to China, for the time being. In every sport, rivalry can push athletes to their limit. The rise of China also meant there were more opportunities for professional players regardless of their nationality to compete on the world stage. In the past, Japan and Korea were the Big 2 that hosted most of the international competitions. With China organizing large-scale international championships and starting its own professional leagues, professional Go players had more exposure to international experience. Quite a few Korean players were already playing in the Chinese major and minor leagues and were enjoying a huge success. They were celebrities with annual pays ranging from tens of millions to hundreds of millions won. Nobody but Jimmy foresaw that such enormous change was imminent.

Since the early 1980s, whenever the occasion arose, Jimmy has open-
ly said that the fate of world Go depended on the success of the Chinese
Go. Jimmy became deeply involved in efforts to promote Go in China
even before the Chinese government gave any form of support. In the
mid-1980s, the Korea Baduk Association wanted to start a meaningful
exchange with its Chinese counterpart but to no avail. Diplomatic ties
between Korea and the Communist China did not exist nor was there any
channel to communicate with each other. The Korea Baduk Association
thought of Jimmy who had immigrated to the U.S. and had become a U.S.
citizen. He seemed to have the perfect profile to be the intermediary for
Korea and China.

Jimmy was asked to meet with the representative of the Chinese Weiqi
Association as the special envoy. He met chairman Chen Zude to talk
about potential partnership. Their first meeting ended without any promises because the Chinese government was adamant about strictly forbid-
ding any form of exchanges between the two parties. But it did plant a
seed of hope in Jimmy's heart. The encounter moved Jimmy to want to
help the Chinese take professional Go in China to the next level. Jimmy
paid out of his own pocket to invite one top player each from Korea and
China to play in California, U.S., in 1985. This match became known as
the 'Korea-China Match.' I was grateful to represent Korea against Nie
Weiping who played for China. Simply put, it was a historical event. For
an individual to successfully pull off a self-organized exchange before

diplomatic ties had even been established was sensational. But Jimmy did not stop there. He wanted to do more. He had a bigger picture in his mind.

"Go must thrive in China to keep international Go moving forward. For more people around the world to fall in love with this brain sport, the game has to gain more popularity and prominence in China."

Back then, no one in Korea understood what Jimmy was talking about because the Korean Go community itself was struggling day-to-day to survive. For many, Jimmy was the lucky guy with the financial resources who could afford to fantasize about the future of Go. A few years later when I met Jimmy, he was busy organizing a big title match in China. Jimmy was going to contribute 60,000 yuan directly to the pool of prize money. At the time in China, prize money ranged from 5,000 or 10,000 yuan at most. Even if a player wins the prize money, 90% went to the Chinese Weiqi Association as tax, leaving only 10% for the player.

Jimmy made a deal with the Chinese Weiqi Association. He offered to sponsor a championship cup in China with a prize money pool of one million yuan including 60,000 yuan set aside for the winner under one condition; the Chinese Weiqi Association was never to claim any of the prize money and the appearance fee. Jimmy was also willing to pay the Chinese Weiqi Association to cover for the preparation that went into organizing the championship. They had no reason to reject such a generous offer.

"We need to offer hefty prize money to professional players to entice young geniuses to the game," said Jimmy to Chen Zude.

That was the beginning of Jimmy's Friendship Cup. The Friendship

Cup was important at two different levels. It instilled a sense of pride in professional Go players as their reputation improved befitting the colossal size of the prize money. It was also a learning experience for the Chinese Weiqi Association to facilitate further progress of Go in China. The Chinese Go players welcomed the Friendship Cup with much enthusiasm. Players thronged the Friendship Cup. Among the 140 were star players like Nie Weiping, Ma Xiaochun, who later ranked 1st in China in the 1990s after Nie Weiping, and Liu Xiaoguang, another world-class player of the 1990s.

The Friendship Cup lasted from 1995 to 1997, during which it was held three times. I had the honor of being invited to the gala evenings and each time I was moved by the very devotion of my dear friend Jimmy. Jimmy was an incredible man. He had big ideas and a bigger heart for Go. I have never seen anyone who was more than happy to mobilize his own resources unconditionally for the benefit of others. I felt the depth of his love for the game of Go.

The Friendship Cup was short-lived but it had a great ripple effect in the Chinese Go community. In 1998, immediately following the last Friendship Cup, the inaugural Chunlan Cup World Professional Weiqi Championship with 150,000 US dollar prize money was held. The overall prize money for local competitions in China made a huge jump. It was around this time that the game received more public attention and the professional Go league gained full-scale traction. Though it lasted for only three years, the Friendship Cup left a significant footprint in the history of the Chinese Go.

The Chinese Go now stands firm on its own feet without any need for external support. It has become the visible big hand in international Go, hosting major large-scale international championships, while internally China's professional league continues to flourish with its own momentum. The rise of the Chinese Go was intimidating to Korean Go but I felt it was a necessary growing pain. Korean professional Go players would have had to worry about their livelihood without the opportunities offered in the growing Go market in China.

The era of Chinese dominance will continue for the time being. But I also believe that Korea and Japan will not just sit back and watch important opportunities pass by. Korea and Japan will work hard to turn the current crisis into an opportunity. Who knows? We may be surprised by the debut of a fresh face- a genius who shifts the paradigm of the existing landscape of Go. And this genius may come from other countries like the U.S., Russia, the EU, or North Korea.

Should one be intimidated by or feel envious of the growth of one's rivals? No. Acknowledge and accept their success. Learn from their experience and build one's own stepping stone to become more competitive. Bigger stages and huge opportunities will come along the way.

I returned to Korea after studying Go in Japan for 9 years. I was waiting to be enlisted to do the mandatory military service. One day, a reporter who was also a close friend of mine, came up to me cautiously.

"Look, I just got the news that Master Segoe passed away…"

What? What did he say? I could not believe it. It had only been 4 months since I left Japan. Master Segoe was over 80 years old, so he was frail, but not fragile.

"How… How did he pass away?"

"Don't be surprised, Hunhyun. Master Segoe, he killed himself."

I came over all faint and dizzy. My legs folded under me.

Next day, every major newspaper in Korea covered the story of Master Segoe's suicide. Master Segoe chose to end his life by strangling himself with his two hands. His body was neat and clean, and two suicide notes were found next to the body; one for his daughter-in-law, Mama zzang, and another one for his friends. Master Segoe wrote to his daughter-in-law that he decided to take his own life because he could not stand being the old man that needed to be looked after constantly. In the other letter, Master Segoe asked his friends and colleagues to bring Kunken back to Japan, and to give him all the necessary support to become a Master of Go. Master Segoe called me Kunken, by my Japanese name.

I was not allowed to leave the country prior to completing my military service. So I asked the people from the Korean Go community who were going to Japan to pay their respects to the deceased to pass my letter of condolence to Mama zzang. There was nothing else I could do. A few weeks later, I went to the army.

The training in the boot camp was arduous. It helped me to endure the shock and the grief of Master Segoe's death. In fact, it had not hit me yet. I could picture him greeting me in his kimono, sitting on the toenmaru like a painting if I paid him a visit to his old house in Japan. Two months later, I received a letter from Mama zzang when I was stationed at the Seongnam airfield.

"Dear Kunken, Benkei passed away a few days ago. He was very depressed since you left to Korea and he stopped eating at all after father passed away. He seemed to have lost the reason to live as two of his masters he loved so much left him one by one. Without you, father and Benkei, I find it unbearable to be the only one left in this empty house......."

I collapsed. It suddenly hit me that Master Segoe and Benkei were gone. Tears poured down my face. Benkei was a black Akita Master Segoe got me when I was 16 to keep me company. Benkei was a small 3-months-old puppy when he came to our house but he grew quickly into a full-size dog. Every day, I started my routine by cleaning up the mess Benkei had made in the yard and walking him around the neighborhood. Benkei was very loyal to me that he followed me everywhere and barked at any stranger who came near me to protect me. An Akita lives up to a decade or longer on average so I could not believe Benkei was already gone. Perhaps he was too sad from losing his two masters.

The news of Benkei's death reminded me of Master Segoe's suicide. It was only then that I began to realize what Master Segoe felt when he had lost me. And the sense of loss had thrown him into deep mourning. Master Segoe was terribly shaken when I was forced to return to Korea to do my mandatory military service. I had never seen him look so confused. He wrote to the Korea Baduk Association and the Military Manpower Administration in Korea to complain about the draft. He pulled every string he could in the Korean political community for help. He tried everything he could. But to his despair, nothing worked.

In the morning when I said my farewell to my Master, I noticed the sadly vacant expression in his eyes. His eyes seemed to be saying that there was nothing to hope for any more. The look of relinquishment. That was the last look of my Master that I remember.

Master Segoe chose to strangle himself to death with his two hands. Most who attempt to end their own lives in this way are likely to let go before they suffocate to death because it is too painful. But nothing could stop Master Segoe. That was the kind of man he was. Once he made up his mind about something, he saw it through.

I was told that Master Segoe lived in complete seclusion after I left. He never went out the house. He was so devastated that he could hardly eat or talk. He was heard murmuring to himself once.

"It must take at least five years for Kunken to come back ...."

Five years was too long for Master Segoe. He was not sure he could wait that long. At a time when he was heartbroken, his close friend, Yasunari Kawabata, left him. Yasunari, who was a Nobel literature laureate, suddenly committed suicide by putting a gas tube in his mouth. His death could have been the trigger for my master's suicide. Master Segoe left, perhaps to accompany his friend.

I did not realize how much Master Segoe loved me until I heard the tragic news of his suicide. I was a student who had no idea how much I was loved by my teacher. Master Segoe never articulated his love for me. It was all embedded in him. And I did not have the maturity to realize the power of his love that was kept inside him all those years.

I am not in the position to judge Master Segoe's decision to commit suicide. What I intend to do is to remember what he left for me. I shall inherit his love for Go and his disciplined and deep mind.

Master Segoe devoted his entire life to the game of Go. His country, his people, his honor, his personal interests were all second to Go. It was his idea to bring Go Seigen from China and train him to become the kind of player who would surprise the Japanese Go community with an exciting disbelief. It was also Master Segoe who made the arrangement for me to study under him and play professional Go on the world stage. Master Segoe would have also done very well for him in the academia or the arts. I was told that he was intelligent as a boy and was a high-achiever. Master Segoe was also an extraordinary amateur painter and calligrapher. His exquisite artwork became well-known and traded at high value in Japan.

Master Segoe played Go well enough to study in Honinbo House, which was one of the four major Go houses in Japan. But he chose to join the Hohenscha[1] , which was a strong rival of the Honinbo House back then because he thought it was important to keep the rivalry going between Honinbo and Hohenscha to ensure that the overall level of Go in Japan remain competitive. In 1908, Master Segoe joined Hohenscha in.

Master Segoe's game record was amazing. In just a few months, he had a total of 39 rounds of games with 30 wins, 6 defeats, and three incomplete. In 1910, he played with Nohsawa 4P, who was frequently called by his nickname, the ghost-like general, because he was notorious for being vituperative to other players. "Your game style is so tacky that I'm demotivated to play," spat out Nohsawa. Master Segoe felt so insulted and mortified that he had to excuse him to the restroom to shed a few tears. He collected himself together and returned to the game, bulldogging it through and beating Nohsawa.

Master Segoe played against Master Honinbo Shusai, the last successor of the hereditary title, Honinbo, during which two handicaps were given. That game became a legend. In the past, when the compensation rule did not exist, handicaps were given to begin with an even game and keep the game even. Master Segoe won 11 rounds in a row when he played against the famous Shusai, and had his handicap adjusted two notches up. The fact that his handicap was adjusted twice meant there was a wide gap in their skill levels. Master Segoe earned 3P from this match, but Nihon Ki-in issued a new rule that readjusting back the game record of every player. This decision was faced with fierce resistance from many players who decided to withdraw from the Japan Go Association, except for Master Segoe. Master Segoe accepted the decision of the Japan Go Association believing it was more important to have a united Go community. To him, the right-or-wrong debate was not worthy of risking the solidarity of the Go community.

Since then, Master Segoe focused solely on training young players. Master Segoe's first student was Utaro Hashimoto who was respected for being gifted in Go and had a great personality that was no less than that of his teacher, Master Segoe. Hashimoto formerly belonged to the Kansai office of Nihon Ki-in but he was not happy with how the Association was wielding authoritarian influence over its members. Utaro decided to co-found Kansai Ki-in with other professional players from the Kansai office who felt the same way. Since its foundation, Kansai Ki-in has functioned as one of the two major associations that led the Japanese Go community. Kansai Ki-in's clout in the Go community abated when Hashimoto passed away, but even today it is still the cradle of talented players like Satoshi Yuki, winner of the Judan Title Match and the Tengen Title Match. Daisuke Murakawa who was the champion of the 2013 Agon Cup was also trained at Kansai Ki-in.

Go Seigen became Master Segoe's second student. Go Seigen was admired for his liberal mind and outstanding leadership that was deemed ahead of his time. Master Segoe went out of his way to bring the young Go Seigen to Japan. Master Segoe and Go Seigen exchanged more than 50 letters over the two years that took to make the arrangement to bring Go Seigen to Japan. Master Segoe reached out to Inukai Tsuyoshi, the then Prime Minister of Japan, who was also known as an avid Go player, to help him invite the young Go Seigen to Japan.

"What are you going to do if the boy later extorts the Meijin Championship Title from Japanese players?" The Prime Minister asked.

"That is exactly what he has to do," replied Master Segoe.

The young Go Seigen developed into a competitive player by leaps and bounds under Master Segoe and rose above every professional player in Japan. The 19-year-old Go Seigen was the first to dared to challenge Master Honinbo Shusai with a new opening. Another well-known episode involves Go Seigen playing the 'mirror game' with Minoru Kitani, where he copied his counterpart's every move during the game. The story behind devising the 'mirror game' was that Go Seigen found Kitani nearly impossible to defeat. In the 'mirror game,' Go Seigen placed his stone symmetrical to the position where Kitani placed his. Go Seigen was not scared of being called a coward for mirroring Kitani. He just wanted to find out how the game would unfold. The Go Seigen vs Kitani game continued into the 62nd move. Go Seigen seemed to turn the table around at one point but he slipped, letting Kitani win the game by three points.

The 'mirror game' brought Go Seigen and Kitani closer like brothers. Together, they invented the innovative new opening pattern called 'Shinfuseki,' which was published as a book entitled, "The Revolutionary Opening Strategy for Go," which completely transformed the way Go was played in Japan. Kitani was 25 and Go Seigen was only 20 at the time. Go Seigen later defeated Kitani in the spectacular series of Jubango matches and every one of his contemporaries. Master Segoe retired when Go Seigen became the undisputed number one player in the country. He gave his own house to Go Seigen while he himself rented a small room and moved out. Master Segoe stopped accepting students until we met 20 years later.

Master Segoe's legacy lives on through the history of the Japanese Go. The Chinese-borne Go Seigen endured through all disadvantages imposed on him because of his nationality. But he was the one who inherited Master Segoe's spiritual heritage and succeeded in becoming the first ranking player in Japan. Today, Go Seigen is one of the players most respected by the Japanese public as evident in his nickname, 'Go Saint.' Go Seigen paid it forward; he taught and trained Rin Kaiho from Taiwan to become the best of the best in Japan. Go Seigen took in Rui Naiwei, who was expelled from the Chinese Weiqi Association, and provided the necessary protection. In 2000, when Rui defeated me and became the first woman in Korea and the world to earn the title of Guksu, Go Seigen was heard saying, "I owe it to Mr. Cho Hunhyun."

As for me, I contemplated on how to continue the legacy of Master Segoe. I met Changho in 1984. I believed it was the opportunity for me to redirect what I have been graciously given to someone as talented as Changho. I knew it was too early for me to accept a student but I did not want to miss the opportunity. I accepted Changho with no strings attached; there was no exchange of a written agreement, not to mention a single penny of tuition fee. Changho was already the perfect candidate when he came to me; he was talented and had the right mindset and the attitude to become successful. I thought I was lucky to have him as my student. Little did I know that the 10-year-old Changho would become a full-sized tiger at 15 and covet my place. Meeting Changho was experiencing both heaven and hell.

If I had only waited for a few more years before taking in Changho, and if Changho's learning curve had only been more gradual, we could have avoided being tangled in an awkward and complicated rivalry and kept our teacher-student relationship simple and easy. Our mentor-mentee relationship posed a challenge we both had to overcome. We did endure and we did come out on the other end of the tunnel safe and relieved. And today, I am proud that Changho carries on, and will continue to carry on, the legacy of Master Segoe, Utaro Hashimoto, Go Seigen, Rin Kaiho, Rui Naiwei, and mine. In this pedigree of Go masters, Changho is the one with the singular radiance. Changho is my legacy.

But my work is not done yet. The legacy of Master Segoe is to keep giving. Now that I am preparing to retire, I spend more time thinking of leaving a legacy. I do not know what it is going to be. I could train another gifted young mind, or I could start a project that could in some way contribute to the Korean Go community. Whatever it may be, I do hope it leaves a lasting footprint and be remembered as a good legacy. I hope I remain strong enough to do my best to leave a legacy. I also hope lady luck on my side.

MASTER'S LEGACY 1977

One autumn day in 1977, the phone rang. It was Master Shuko.

"Kunken, I'm at the Gimpo Airport. Come and get me quickly."

It was a pleasant surprise. Master Shuko came without any notice. I did not know what to say but I could feel a smile spreading across my face. It was so typical of Master Shuko!

I found Master Shuko waving his hand and shouting my name "KunKen" as I was arriving at the airport. He looked half-sober, half-drunk. Master Shuko was wearing a sloppy shirt and pants. He came without any luggage except for a bottle of Santori beer that was sticking out of his back pocket. He was so delighted to see me that he gave me a quick hard squeeze.

"Master Shuko! How did you get here?"

"I came to see you, of course."

Master Shuko got on the first flight on impulse. He was drinking until dawn and suddenly realized he missed me very much.

"Kunken, my boy! You will get into trouble with me if you have been lazy playing Go!"

Master Shuko and I went straight to check-in to a hotel near the Cheonggye creek and we did not leave our room for three days. We spent most of the time playing Go and going over game records, occasionally being interrupted by guests from the Korean Go community who came to say hello to Master Shuko. We also played a few quick games and Master

Shuko made me rub his stiff shoulders and arms every time I lost. Master Shuko took the time to look at every game record I had accumulated.

Master Shuko did not stop drinking for three whole days. He also did not stop analyzing and evaluating my game records even when he was as drunk as a fish. He did not get tired at all whereas I was exhausted from playing and analyzing for three days straight and I only had mineral water to drink. I was wondering how such a small man could be so strong.

"I was going to scold you if your skills had deteriorated. But I am relieved that you still play well. Now I can go home."

If Master Segoe was the head coach, Master Shuko was the technical skills coach. I learned to play Go from Master Segoe but I was also a member of the Fujisawa study group too. I was a 12-year-old Go prodigy at the Japan Go Association when I met Master Shuko for the first time. We ran into each other and played a round of game. Master Shuko invited me to come to his study group after the game. Ever since that day, Master Shuko became my second mentor. Master Shuko was always surrounded by a lot of people. Rin Kaiho, Koichi Kobayashi, Cho Chikun and I went to his study group to play Go whenever we could. The study group was always on the move because Master Shuko never had enough to afford a permanent place. But that did not matter to us. When it was time to move, we carried the game boards and the office furniture ourselves to the new place. We never got tired of moving.

Master Shuko had a singular reputation that was second to none. If Master Segoe was ascetic, Master Shuko was eccentric that he earned the nickname, 'Shuko, the monster.' Unlike the ordinary people whose manner was civil and polite, Master Shuko did not hesitate to behave in unconventional ways. He was also candid and an open-book. He was someone who had flaws but he was irresistibly adorable. Master Shuko used to visit China with members of his study group in the 1980s. On one occasion, he was invited to a banquet hosted by Deng Xiaoping, the late leader of China. The banquet was interrupted when Master Shuko got drunk and became too loud. If the source of fuss had been someone else, that individual would have been in a big trouble, but Master Shuko had the ability to make people fall in love with him and forgive his rough edges.

Master Shuko was a man who had the charming naivety and the free spirit of a child. He has so much love in him. He drank like a fish and loved women as much as he loved those who were his junior. He loved gambling as much as he loved playing Go. Master Shuko treated those who were his junior like his peers. He never let his authority as an established professional player to come between him and the younger players. His affection for the talented players did not know national boundaries. He cared for Korean players like Cho Chikun and myself, as well as Chinese players like Nie Weiping.

In the 1989 Ing Cup, Master Shuko, Nie Weiping, Rin Kaiho, and myself- a.k.a. Shuko's entourage, advanced into the semifinals. It was amazing that Master Shuko made it to the semifinals considering that he was over 60 back then. But what was even more unbelievable was the level of his tranquility and confidence. Before the semifinals, I heard Master Shuko saying, "Cho Hunhyun is the best in the world. The Ing Cup is going to be his. I might meet him at the finals though."

Master Shuko had the sense of humor to self-praise by praising me.

Master Shuko also cared about Changho because he thought of Changho as his 'grand-student' since Changho was my student. Master Shuko wrote a letter to Changho when the Korean team won the 1994 Jinro Championship Cup. Changho was the captain of the Korean team. Master Shuko started by congratulating Changho on the achievement and went on to remind Changho about his philosophy of the game and the virtues that befits the best player in the world. Master Shuko's letter was filled with warmth and affection for his 'grand-student.'

"I was very much impressed by Cho Hunhyun, who was just a little boy back then. I believed that he might be the most talented Go player in the whole world. When you defeated Cho Hunhyun, Mother Nature was probably taking its own course, but I was sad thinking that even the best could not defy Mother Nature. For one reason or another, I was looking forward to playing a game with you, and that wish came true at the Fujistu Cup in April. You won but I was not quite happy with your style. I did not like how you played the game one bit. It may be something you need to work on. You play like a professional but with no emotions. Your game is barely inspiring. The game of Go is not just a sport that one needs to win; it is a form of art, just like music or painting, with which one expresses one's unique individuality. In order for it to be a work of art, it needs to have a creative and unique aspect that can speak to us. Go is not just about winning. More importantly, it is about expressing oneself. A world champion owes that much to the game. Keep working hard because I will do my best to train young Japanese players so they could beat you."

Lee Changho was deeply moved by Master Shuko's letter that he included the full text of the letter in his autobiography, "Greed for Victory Takes It Away." It was Changho's way of expressing his will to follow Master Shuko's words.

Master Shuko's indomitable will earned him the nickname, 'monster.' He led an undeterred freewheeling life. He was a freeman who indulged himself in drinking and having affairs with the ladies. He also ran through his fortune betting on horse racing as well as bicycle race. But he always managed to get back on his feet again. He had an invincible spirit. Master Shuko was between a rock and debt when he was playing in the 2nd Kisei Title Match. Before he headed for the play room, he found a tree suitable to hang himself. Master Shuko made one move after 2 hours 57 minutes and he succeeded in catching his opponent's big stone group and finished off the game. It was his second victory in that match. Master Shuko defended the Kisei Title by winning two more rounds afterwards. He had an unbroken string of victories to the 7th Kisei Title Match that he paid off his remaining debts.

Master Shuko suffered from three different types of cancers that included malignant lymphoma and prostate cancer after he went through gastrectomy to treat gastric cancer in his late 50s. Yet, he never stopped teaching, drinking, and marring and divorcing quite a number of wives. In 1992, Master Shuko won the 40th Oza Title Match at the age of 67. He will probably go down in the history of Japanese Go as the oldest winner of a championship title and I have a feeling that the record will not be rewritten any soon.

Master Shuko died of pneumonia in 2009. One month before his death, he was still running his study group and was welcoming anyone to the group who was interested in Go. Master Shuko's students from Korea, China, and Japan gathered at his funeral to mourn and to pay tribute to him. We remembered how he did not spare a penny for whomever he was fond of. He was a man of big heart who happily did others' favors. He deeply cared about the talented young players. He drank as much as he pleased and slept rough whenever he was not sober enough to find his way back home. That was who Master Shuko Fujisawa was.

Master Shuko's real name was Hideyuki Fujisawa. In fact, only the heir to the Honinbo House was allowed to use "Shu" in their name. Master Shuko was not an heir to the Honinbo House, but his students began to call him 'Shuko' out of respect and affection for him, and the Japan Go Association agreed to acknowledge 'Shuko Fujisawa' as his official name.

Even now, when I think of Master Shuko, I remember him as a giver. He had a big heart that could embrace hundreds of students including myself. He was always brimming with abundant love. The world might remember him as the player who lived a tumultuous life, but I remember him as the man who was madly in love with the world.

How many people is my heart capable of holding? Am I capable of falling madly in love with the world? No matter how hard I try, I may never be able to follow in his footsteps. I only wish I could offer my best to others, just as he offered me his everything. Today, I shall continue my open-minded and open-hearted endeavors.

"Youth is a blessing.

It is what makes the young great.

The dilemma, however, is that it does not last forever."

Chapter 8

Train
the Body
for the Mind

GOODBYE, ROSE

I used to be a heavy smoker a long time ago. Every day, I smoked four to five packs on average, which means I was always lighting up cigarettes when I was awake. I preferred the brand, 'Jangmi,' which meant 'rose' in Korean. Rose was a cheap slim cigarette, one of the mildest out there in the market back then. But, no matter how mild it was, cigarette is still cigarette. It must have done more harm than good to any chain smoker.

Unlike today, playing Go professionally meant taking up smoking in the old days. I cannot remember when and how I began to play Go, but I do remember that I was always surrounded by cigarette smoke. My father used to play Go on the second floor of this building which was always thick with cigarette smoke. The first Go club that my father took me to, the one in the city of Mokpo, was no exception. I could smell the stale odor of the cigarette smoke as soon as I stepped into the club. As the only boy in the club, I became in charge of buying cigarettes for the grown-ups. In my defense, it was natural for me to pick up a cigarette as soon as I turned into an adult because I grew up watching grown-ups smoke in the club. Smoking seemed part of being an adult.

For my wife, Mihwa, having a chain-smoking husband was something she just had to live with, the fate of a professional Go player's wife, so to speak. Worrying for my health or nagging me to quit smoking was not something the wife of a professional Go player could afford to do. The usual four to five packs a day became five to six, or even seven packs a day when I was competing. Mihwa would then, open the windows to let fresh air in and she would be constantly going in and out of my room to empty the ashtray. Instead of nagging me to cut down on cigarettes, Mihwa used to order dozens of boxes of Jangmi- each box containing 10,000 cigarettes- and store them in the basement.

Heavy smoking took its toll on me. I came down with a cold accompanied by swollen tonsils every time I was about to have an important competition. I began to suspect that it had something to do with smoking but it never occurred to me that I had to quit smoking. Smoking had become part of my life and I could not give it up until one day I was forced to make up my mind about it. It was in the mid-1990s when I paid a visit to my long-time friend, Jimmy in the U.S. I had said 'hi' to Jimmy who came to pick me up at the airport and I was just about to light a cigarette as I got into his car.

"No smoking in my car!" Jimmy blurted out and I could see that he was serious.

I put away my cigarette but I was furious inside. I had to fight my cravings for tobacco during the entire flight to the U.S. and I realized I was not getting one any soon. Jimmy's car was not the only smoke-free zone. I found the 'no smoking' sign wherever I went- restaurants, shopping malls, banks, and gas stations. People gave me the dirty look even in parking lots. Worse, I got stared at as if I were committing a serious crime if there happened to be kids around when I was smoking.

"Where on earth am I allowed to smoke?"

I exploded in anger.

"Well, you can quit smoking," said Jimmy.

In a fit of rage, I took out the pack of cigarettes from my pocket, crumbled it, and tossed it into a trash can.

"I would rather quit than to have people make me feel guilty about smoking my own cigarette!"

That was how I came about to quit smoking. I was already half way through giving up smoking entirely when I came back to Korea. Mihwa was excited than anybody else. She was more than happy to throw away all the cigarette boxes that were stored in the basement. My children were happy too because they no longer had to put up with the smell of tobacco. And strange things began to happen.

I got my appetite back. I have always had a poor appetite so it was not unusual for me to not be able to finish a bowl of rice. But, not only did I finish my bowl of rice, I asked for more after I quit smoking. My craving did not end with a bowl of rice. I had never eaten anything between meals before but I started to snack and I could not help wanting more of everything. I finished a plateful dried anchovy Mihwa gave me for a light snack. I even cleaned the plate that was full of cookies for kids. Mihwa started to get busy to fill my stomach. She made me old school Korean snacks and beverages, such as the yakgwa (honey cookie), yugwa (deep-fried sweet rice puff), gangjeong (fried sticky rice crackers with nuts), yeot (hard taffy Korean-style), sikhye (sweet rice punch), and sujeonggwa (cinnamon punch). They were all delicious and it was only then that I realized what a great cook she was.

I began to see improvements in my appearance, too. When I was smoking, I was a mere walking skeleton, so skin-and-bones that my frame accentuated the cheekbones. My skin looked dark and dull, too. After I quit smoking, I started to put on weight which softened my facial contour. My skin tone became lighter and brighter. I was surprised when I got on the scale. I had added 10kg in a short time. People saw my transformation when I showed up at competitions and I became the talk of the town. Cho Hunhyun gave up smoking! Smoking was his middle name! There were rampant speculations over why I decided to give up smoking. It was rumored that I had given up on smoking to gain greater self-control in order to perform better. Some major newspapers even covered my story writing headlines such as, 'The Fighter's Firm Resolution,' and 'Turning Over a New Leaf: Cho Hunhyun Quits Smoking.' It was probably a coincidence that I happened to quit smoking around the time I had lost my Guksu Title to Changho for the second time around. It was the perfect timing for the media to make the connection between the two events so I did not see any point in trying to correct them.

Anyway, quitting smoking actually helped me play better. There had been remarkable improvement in my physical strength. I have had to lean back in a chair from a stiff neck, shoulders, and back to get through a round of game, not to mention lose concentration half-way through the game. But I felt comfortable the entire time I was playing a game after I quit smoking. So I came to admit that age was not the sole cause of my ever-weakening endurance. I had been torturing my body by feeding it all kinds of bad chemicals. Once the poisonous substances that had been accumulating in my system for the past two decades disappeared, I started to feel lighter, I could concentrate better, and I was more relaxed at competitions.

Quitting smoking was not something I had planned on but its benefits had changed me physically and mentally, as well as how I played games. Giving up smoking had also become the trend. Not long after I stopped smoking, a movement started within the Go community in Korea to make rooms used for competitions smoke-free. With the average age of those passing the Professional Qualification Tournament getting younger, more people were arguing for prohibiting smoking altogether while playing Go. Even highly-revered 9P players were not to be exempted from the non-smoking rule because of the consensus that smoking could cause grave danger to the health of young players if they are exposed to second-hand smoking. For a while when the change was being introduced, the rooms used for the preliminary rounds were divided into smoking and non-smoking rooms. It worked when both of the players were either smokers or non-smokers but the problem arose when a smoker and a non-smoker played against each other. If the game was held in the smoking room, the non-smoker suffered from cigarette smoke. On the other hand, the challenge for a smoker in the non-smoking room was to bring his craving for a cigarette under control, which was deemed the right thing to do as well as less painful than having a non-smoker endure the cigarette smoke in the smoking room.

In 1999, The Korea Baduk Association decided that all rooms used for competitions were to be smoke-free zones. Today, no one is allowed to smoke in the competition rooms anymore. On rare occasions, a player or two may quietly step out in the hallway for a quick smoke. Go clubs in suburban areas have a designated smoking room. A Go club that is filled with cigarette smoke has become a thing of past. Sometimes with the smell of a whiff of cigarette, old memories of the Go club would rush back, making me feel nostalgia about the good old days. Don't get me wrong, it is not the cigarette that I miss because I even shake my head sideways in disapproval, wondering how I did wrong to myself, inhaling bad chemicals into my own body.

Immediately after I quit smoking, I found myself competing more frequently and winning back the LG Cup World Baduk Championship, the Paewang Title Match, and the BC Card Cup World Baduk Championship. People said giving up smoking made all of that possible. But I believe that breakthrough had more to do with regaining my physical and mental health than quitting smoking.

GO: THE SAD BUT HOPEFUL DRAMA

The level of my endurance was at par with younger players until I reached 45. But I seemed to have hit my limit in 2001 when I was playing in the Wangwi Title Match. I got off to a quick start winning five games in a row. But I ended up losing by half a point to Seo Bongsoo 9P because I mixed up the compensation rule of the Wangwi Title Match with that of another tournament. It was entirely my fault. I should have checked the rules of the Wangwi Title Match because they were different for every competition. As a result, I had to play extra rounds to break the tie with Bongsoo. Things could not have been worse when the preliminary rounds of the Fujitsu Cup World Go Championship fell right on the same time. I spent 10 days playing 6 games in both tournaments. I advanced into the final by a narrow margin as the contender of the Wangwi Title but I knew I did not have any energy left to stay in the game. Regrettably, I did not make it to the first round of the finals held in Haenam. I was confined to my sick bed, suffering from high fever and complete exhaustion. Changho, who was defending the title, was at a loss of words when I withdrew from the tournament, making him the winner without having to lift a finger. I believe I was the first and the last contender in the history of Korean Go to give up and thereby lose. I did manage to get out of bed but I had not fully recovered yet. I did not get to finish the second and the third rounds, which were held few days apart, because I resigned in the middle of the game. I got as far as the 75th move in the third round until

I decided to give up. This game became the quickest defeat in the history of a contending match.

I was playing against Yoo Changhyuk 9P in the finals of the 6th LG Cup World Baduk Championship in 2002. Changhyuk had just returned from a tournament held in Japan and he seemed to be exhausted. He never got around to start a momentum and he expressed his resignation. I thought it had to do with his age because he was almost 40. Suddenly, I came down with the flu on the following day and I got extremely sick. I lost the fourth and the fifth rounds to Changhyuk and finished second in the tournament.

So that is how it feels to be old. In my youth, I was able to keep up with the tight and hectic competition schedules while chainsmoking but it was not the case anymore. If I overstretched myself, I got sick and had to stay in bed for days. I also made mistakes that I never made when I was young. For example, I thought I was making a counterattack but realized that I was making the wrong move all along. Sometimes I miscalculated the scores which made me assume I was winning when in fact I ended up losing. The images of the sequences that used to come to my mind crystal-clear were now blurred and distorted making me fumble with the stones and creating a mass on the board. These strange symptoms seemed to be the outcome of aging and weakening strength.

They were less obtrusive when I was still playing at a certain level despite the errors. A week after my hopeless defeat at the 2001 Wangwi Title Match, I won the 14th Fujistu Cup World Go Championship. In the following year, I played against Changhyuk 9P and finished runner-up at the LG Cup World Baduk Championship. Fortunately, I won the next tournament, which was the KT Cup and the Samsung Fire & Marine Insurance World Masters Baduk. In 2003, I also made it to the finals of the Wangwi Title Match and the Kisung Title Match where I finished second. I was commended for performing at par with the younger players in my 50s.

But I am only human after all. How could a mortal being defy the test of time? I began to head downhill in 2003. My name was no longer heard in both local and international tournaments. I was rarely mentioned in anything related to Go that people assumed I had retired. I was still playing tirelessly, just not in the high-profile tournaments.

Winning is a mysterious thing. It feels like yesterday that I was fiercely competing to be the champion even if by half a point. My mind was sharp and my skills honed but they did not last forever. After all these years, I realized that youth is the best ammunition. The time comes when the experiences and the know-hows an old man had accumulated over time lose their edge to the energy and the ambition of a young man. Youth wins, therefore, youth is ominous.

Perhaps that is life and the law of nature. In the end, the elderly king is forced to abdicate to pass the throne to the younger and stronger prince. Eio Sakata 9P, the "razor" and the "fighting spirit" who won championship titles 64 times in Japan in the 1960s, lost both the Meijin and the Honinbo titles to Rin Kaiho, who was his junior. The night he lost to Rin

Kaiho, Eio was said to have lamented over a drink.

"I was just starting to get to know the real Go at 40, but it is over now. What a sad ending."

This sad drama of Go is constantly replayed as if governed by the law of nature. Master Shuko had to give up the Kisei Title to Cho Chikun who, in turn, later failed to defend the Oza and Kisei Titles against the Taiwanese contender, O Rissei. I lost all of my titles to my student, Changho, and Changho lost his to his junior, Sedol. Sedol is now facing tough challenges from his junior players.

Time is unkind and heartless, as they say and I agree. It is sad to see how things change with time. But it is only natural that time flows like the four seasons that alternate. There is no reason to feel hurt by the fact that it leaves no room for human intervention. Everyone gets to be young once in their lifetime. We get to enjoy it to the fullest so there is no reason to be jealous of the young. Those who are at the height of their youth today and boast of being young will lose it, too, one day.

The end of youth does not mean the end of life. Life replaces youth with many perks. As for me, I feel liberated from the pressure of having to win which allows me to play more at ease. The moment I admitted that I could be defeated in any given game, I was able to free myself from the fetters of my obsession with winning. Winning was the source of my pride and my identity but it also imprisoned me. Living under unbearable pressure to always win for decades can be torturous. Fortunately, Mother Nature lets time to flow so that it can put an end to our long ordeals and free us from the shackles. Therefore, we must not be sad. We must celebrate with joy.

I look at Changho with mixed feelings. I am sad that he is growing feeble, but I hope he appreciates the relinquishing process. Changho seemed to have skipped his childhood to go straight into playing professional Go. It had always bothered me that he did not get to live a single day as an ordinary child. Chagnho was always surrounded by grown-ups who were 10 to 20 years his senior without having any friends of his own age. Living away from home, he did not get to be spoiled by his parents.

Changho is free now. He is liberated. He met his other half and got married. He does not need to be too serious, fighting with those who are much older than he is. He can continue playing with those in their 20s or 30s, give a big smile if he wins and let out a deep sigh if he loses. He can finally be his age.

I am living my age, too. Like any man in his 60s, I often go for a stroll in my neighborhood, water my garden, and play golf with my Mihwa. I am filling up my calendar with everyday activities I missed out to play at Go tournaments. I would be happy to be a grandpa if my children were to get married now and have their own kids.

But I have not entirely given up on competing. That may be the one thing that I will never give up as long as I live. Age and physical frailty cannot be an excuse in the world of competition. The moment I start making excuses for my poor performance, my life as a fighter will end. I believe I can still win as long as I continue to train to stay in good shape and to stay focused. One can win or lose by a small margin, even by half a point. So it is not a long shot for someone of my age to win. I just need to try a little harder, that is all.

In fact, I have proved that I can still win in the first BC Card Cup World Baduk Championship held in 2009, when I entered as a wild card and made the semifinals. It was the first time I competed in the semifinals after winning the kt Cup and the Samsung Fire & Marine Insurance World Masters Baduk 7 years ago. Although I lost in the BC Card Cup to Gu Li by half a point, I was thrilled as if I was stepping on a thin layer of ice. I missed the thrill.

In 1981, the then 56-year-old Master Shuko had an interview after he won five times in a row in the Kisei Title Match. Master Shuko said, "My brain is ever more agile at 50. I am strategizing with a perspective as broad as the ocean. I am also reading sequences with more precision like a well-calibrated measuring instrument. Watch me. My intellectual ability will continue to soar with the force and the freedom of a charging buffalo in the wilderness."

Master Shuko won the Kisei Title Match 6 times by 1982, and he and I advanced to the semifinals in the Ing Cup in 1989. Master Shuko also won the Oza Title in 1992 when he was 68. Masao Kato redeemed himself by beating players in their 20s and 30s and winning the Honinbo Title at the age of 55 in 2002. Masao had been long forgotten in the world of Go after he won the Oza Title in 1993. He proved that youth was formidable but not invincible.

Young people should make the most of their youth, but refrain from being overconfident about it. They must be humble. Youth is a blessing. It is what makes the young great. The dilemma, however, is that it does not last forever. Youth is transitory. The young must be ambitious and must have the will to climb up the ladder to achieve their dreams. But they must also eat healthy, regularly exercise, and train their muscles and mind to relax. In this way, they will be prepared to enjoy a healthy and happy life as they age. Another source of happiness would be to work harder to beat the young once in a while. Never mind if winning is a long shot. The process of working towards a goal is itself meaningful and delightful.

THE HEALING MOUNTAIN

Hiking is part of my daily routine. I would not call it a full-out mountain climbing. Rather, it is walking the trail on a nearby mountain that requires simple preparation, such as putting on a T-shirt, a pair of cotton pants, a pair of boots and wrapping a towel around my neck. My destination is the Bukhansan which is just across my house. I have been mountain hiking every day since 1991, when Changho moved out and we moved to live nearby the Bukhansan in 1991. The only time I missed hiking was to participate in competitions. I have been hiking for over the past two decades.

In fact, I had begun to hike before we moved. I found hiking to be stress-relieving, especially when I was under a lot of pressure to play well. So I decided to start a hiking club with a few close friends who were older than me.

Every Sunday, we used to meet at Jongno 4-ga, downtown Seoul to go to the Dobongsan. We spent the entire day on the mountain, rain or shine. We also made the effort to go to faraway mountains semi-annually or annually, like the Jirisan, the Seoraksan, or the Wolchulsan. As time went by, unfortunately, our hiking club was dissolved for inevitable reasons, such as health issues or relocating away from Seoul. We, too, moved around that time and I started to hike alone.

One-man hiking could get lonely compared to the boisterous group hiking but it had its own benefits. I could be flexible about when I want to go hiking without bothering to make an arrangement with other people. I could hike in the Bukhansan and save time without having to travel to another mountain. I could walk on my own pace; take a rest whenever I got tired or speed up as fast as I could when I feel like it. Sometimes, I could be ambitious and climb all the way to the top, on other times, I could make a quick trip halfway.

But the best part of hiking alone lied in that I could have some time to myself. Of course, I could be alone in my own house, but it felt completely different when I was walking alone in nature. I was able to block out any unwanted noise.

When I was just starting to hike alone, I had so many thoughts in my mind; I was thinking about my tournament schedule, an unresolved move, and games I had won or lost. I was distracted so much so that I had head-aches. But, amidst being out-of-breath and breathing heavy, there came a point when all of the thoughts vanished from my mind. The anxiety of losing and all the trivial things of the daily life were dismissed. I reached a point where I was no longer conscious of myself. In the end, I could only feel my two legs climbing uphill.

I could not explain how, but focusing solely on climbing made me find inner peace. I was sweating and out of breath, but it was not painful. I felt lighter and refreshed.

In retrospect, hiking everyday helped me build the physical strength and the endurance to not only play in over 100 games a year but also do well occasionally even in my 40s and 50s. If you think of Go as a mind sport that entails just sitting through a game and thinking, you are terribly mistaken. Physical strength is critical to stay focused until the last move is made. Physical strength is the basis of everything.

Hiking has also allowed me to make a habit of emptying out petty thoughts from my mind, which helped me to perform better and improve the quality of my life. Taking my mind off the goals and the duties, and relieving stress for an hour a day have the effect of broadening the scope of my perspective. I cannot rise above all, but I can deal with setbacks, distress, and tough times more gracefully.

When the society we live in continues to move forward and urbaniza-tion and globalization go on, we are more likely to become disconnected from Mother Nature. Human beings were designed to walk, move, and work, but we have evolved to work by sitting still for a long time inside a concrete building. We turn to various wheeled means of transportation to move around instead of walking with our own legs fussing over how busy or tired we are. We are affected by the environment we have created without realizing its effect on our mind and body. Why do we suffer from chronic digestion, gastrointestinal disorder, and short temper and fatigue with no specific reason? Why do we feel tired even when we are working sitting at our desks all day long? The answer to these questions is because we spend too much time sitting down. That is all we do instead of walking and running.

Someone who works sitting at the desk needs to make time to walk. Securing time to discard unnecessary thoughts while walking and sweating is a good way to refresh oneself.

It does not have to be hiking. I chose to hike, but it could be jogging, swimming, or playing soccer. The point is to keep the mind and the body in balance with each other. The mind and the body are not separate. They supplement each other and are one. Walking has become more important today because the mind is overworked by heavy workloads, the heavy and extensive use of computers and smartphones. Make the effort to walk at least on weekends, if including it in the daily routine is not feasible. Take a walk to a nearby park or a mountain. Walk until out-of-breath and feel the worries and distractions disappear.

THE DISTRACTING FACTOR

The mobile phone is considered a necessity in today's fast-paced digital world. Everyone has to have one regardless of age and gender. It has evolved into smartphones that allow us to do more than just make phone calls or send text messages. We check our emails, play games, and carry out business transactions on our smartphones.

But I don't own a smartphone, or a feature phone, or a credit card, or a driver's license. I don't have a driver's license because I never learn to drive a car. In Korea, people get their drivers' license in their early 20s. As for me, I did not have the time to get one because I was busy competing in tournaments. In my 30s, I became used to having Mihwa give me a lift. Today, it is my daughter who gives me the ride as Mihwa often does not feel strong enough to drive anymore. I never owned a credit card because I never needed one. Mihwa always made sure I had cash in my wallet. I never got into trouble because I was short of money.

People are amazed at how I can get by without a phone. But I have my own way of keeping in touch with people for important things. First of all, I rarely have the need to make a call. I don't meet a lot of people and when I do, I prefer not to make any adjustments. When people need to make any changes, they can either look for me at home or in the Go club I have often visited. Mihwa receives my messages when I am not home. When nobody's home, people call Mihwa to get in touch with me. It does take time to get messages delivered this way, but even so I have never once missed an important message. Once I was in China for a tournament and I was having lunch at a restaurant. The restaurant told me that I had a call and I was amazed that someone could locate me at the restaurant. It turned out that the person who called got a hold of my wife, who relayed his message to the Go club, which called the hotel I was staying at find my whereabouts. An important message is bound to reach the person it is intended for one way or another.

I do not mean to say that a mobile phone is unnecessary. Life without a mobile phone could be inconvenient but we can still get by. We still met people and sent important messages before the mobile phone was invented. Moreover, we were careful about what we said and we valued promises because it was not easy to get in touch with each other. By contrast, setting up appointments have become so easy and convenient today that people feel it is ok to change their mind all the time. Deep thinking and prudence have lost grounds in the age of digital civilization.

One day, I asked my daughter about the difference between a smartphone and a feature phone. My daughter said that the smartphone allowed her to check her emails in real-time, send group messages, share her stories with people around the world, and make friends. It was certainly amazing what she could do with a smartphone. But I could not help but wonder, 'Why we choose to live in such a way?'

There is no real reason other than the fact that we have the technologies and the devices that allow us to live in such a way. Without the means, we would not have thought they would be possible nor necessary.

How many emails in our inbox require immediate attention? How much of the text messages we exchange are absolutely necessary? How many times have we realized that it was unnecessary to rush to look up a particular information on the internet?

What is more problematic is that we end up running out of time to do what really matters. We run out of time to concentrate on our work or to mediate. The smartphone, the noise from the T.V., the radio, constant chatter, floods of advertisements, and rumors about celebrities distract us from concentrating and meditating. As a result, we no longer have the time to contemplate to the point that we cannot stand silence. So we call or text our friends when we don't have anything important to say, play loud songs, and turn up the volume T.V.

Turn off the mobile phone and the music for at least 10 minutes a day to have undisturbed time to yourself. One does not need to be thinking of huge ideas. Just let the mind take a rest with eyes closed. Everyone needs a quiet downtime to face our inner selves.

The mind cannot think of creative ideas when it is already filled with other thoughts. The mind can brainstorm creative ideas when there is room, or when one has zoned out. Setting some time aside every day to meditate without being distracted will help an individual to be more patient, relaxed, positive, and creative.

I have had to cut off many things from my life to focus on playing Go ever since I was a child. I did not watch the T.V., nor read the newspaper. I also limited my use of phone to a minimum. In this way, I was able to secure ample time to learn Go on my own. I had created a noise-free environment for myself that allowed me to do deep thinking.

We are constantly pressed for time and have become used to leaving things unfinished. We may have brought it upon ourselves by creating an environment that intrudes into our lives; the text alerts, the music, the noise from the T.V. and the constant calls from our friends that claims our time.

ON SOLITUDE

One of the questions reporters used to ask me all the time was, "How do you deal with losing?"

Unfortunately, I don't have the answer simply because all I did was to endure them. There was no such thing as a 'secret recipe.' And time healed.

But I may have an answer if the question is rephrased to, "what did you do after you were defeated?" I chose to be left alone although it was nearly impossible when I had to be at competitions back-to-back. I tried to secure some time alone as much as possible. Sometimes, I spent hours away from my family. I spent time alone in silence and took a break from everything. I found it to be very healing. Then I was ready to walk out the door and face the world again.

Being in solitude is a choice an individual makes voluntarily. The difference between being in solitude and self-isolation is that unlike self-isolation, choosing to withdraw from the crowd allows one to have an honest talk with one's inner self. Therefore, it is not entirely painful nor meaningless.

One must withdraw into solitude in order to achieve one's goals. One thing that successful people share in common is that they spent time alone to overcome their limitation. Masterpieces were created in this way. They would not have been able to sharpen their skills without taking the time to think, meditate and practice in solitude.

People are often distracted by the glamorous side of being successful. They only see how successful people perform at their best and are surrounded by an applauding crowd. They see only the best part. Very few are prepared to see the underlying hard work and dedication of an individual.

Professional Go players live in solitude. Learning how to play the game, competing, accepting, and overcoming the outcome- each is a lonely journey. They rarely have anyone to talk to, or to share what they go through. They deal with their situation alone and find solace in solitude. We willingly withdraw into the dark cave of solitude to become stronger and to overcome the memory of the last defeat.

A philosopher once said, "A strong person is someone who endures loneliness." Another said, "Loneliness is liberating. Loneliness makes one stronger." To gather the wisdom to live by and to make one's dream come true, one must have the maturity that befits the level of one's skills.

One needs to spend more time thinking in solitude.

Go with the Flow